The Lilypad

7 steps to the simple life

by
Marian Van Eyk McCain

FINDHORN
Press

©Marian Van Eyk McCain 2004

First published by Findhorn Press in 2004

ISBN 1-84409-037-X

British Library Cataloguing-in-Publication Data.
A catalogue record for this book is available
from the British Library.

Edited by Kate Keogan
Cover and interior design by Thierry Bogliolo.
Cover photograph © PhotoDisc
Inside illustrations © Iris Hill

Printed and bound by WS Bookwell, Finland

Published by
Findhorn Press
305a The Park, Findhorn
Forres IV36 3TE
Scotland, UK
tel 01309 690582/fax 690036
info@findhornpress.com
www.findhornpress.com

Contents

Beginning

"The Frog Pond"

I shine my torch on the garden pond.

A carpet of duckweed covers almost the entire surface of the water, still and smooth and green as a golf course, broken here and there by the pinnate leaf of a water parsnip.

Around the edges, the honey-coloured rocks are almost hidden now in a tangle of wild plants.

I am searching for snails and slugs. For although they are welcome to feast at will here, in this wild corner of the garden, I cannot risk that some time later tonight they will make the two-metre journey to the place where wildness ends and the cabbage patch begins.

There seem to be neither snails nor slugs abroad here tonight. But the arc of my torch beam catches something else. A pair of eyes, just above the water level. And another, and another..., small faces, still and solemn, under rakish little hats of duckweed.

My pond has frogs again.

I never think to peel back the mat of water parsnip roots and duckweed to look for spawn or tadpoles in the spring. So every year the fully-formed frogs seem to appear from nowhere, as though they had parachuted in from somewhere else. Yet I know they were born here. Deep within the brown-green water of this tiny pond, they hatched and swam and slowly turned themselves from wriggling tadpoles into miniature frogs. Right here, beneath the duckweed and beneath my awareness, their miracle of transformation happened and their amphibian lives began. This is their taken-for-granted world and this, to them, is all the world there is. Beyond the rocks, beyond the nettles, lies the far edge of the Universe.

I swing my torch again and count them. Six pairs of eyes – or is it seven? Ah, there is another, almost hidden in the water parsnips. It feels like one of those "can you find it?" puzzles we loved as children. You stare and stare at the page and suddenly there is a tiger in the undergrowth. Or a frog in the water parsnips. And you wonder how you could have missed it earlier.

They blend in well, their browny-green colours melding with the natural colours of the vegetation. In fact, had it been daylight, I doubt I would have seen them at all. For these frogs are made to fit their surroundings. Only Nature's clever use of camouflage has kept them and their ancestors from the greedy beaks of herons.

Are there herons that would eat us alive, too, if we failed to fit in as well with our surroundings as these frogs fit with theirs?

I think there are. And I think they are already here and hungry. For as far as I am aware, there has never, in the history of our world, been a creature which could survive for very long if it failed to fit in properly with its surroundings. We are the first, foolish animals to try it. And our arrogance may be our undoing.

So the herons of global warming and climate change, the herons of water shortage and of desertification, they and all the other herons will fly in from the outer edges of the Universe and catch and eat us, and the big experiment will be over.

But what if we changed our ways now? Would it be too late?

I don't know. No-one knows. But we can surely try.

This book is to share the discoveries I have made about living properly in one's own small pond, blending in with the rest of Nature, living simply and being happy.

I am not sure if these frogs are happy. Their eyes are unblinking and their tiny faces are inscrutable. But they are still and quiet and living patiently, peacefully and – as far as I can tell – totally in the here and now. I have noticed that, on the odd occasions when I can manage to do that, it seems to bring me a certain kind of happiness which I should like to feel more often – all the time, if possible.

As I walk back down the path, searching for slugs and snails in my torch beam, I am aware of a memory that keeps trying to surface. It seems to be important, but I cannot quite grasp it. Like a dream, forgotten on waking, it has slipped too far over the rim of my consciousness and I cannot haul it back. Never mind. If it is important, I expect it will return.

Introduction – Part One
Why I wrote this book

This book about simplicity is written for two reasons. Firstly, I am now much nearer to the end of my life than to the beginning. So, before I die, I want to share my most important insights about simple living, on the off-chance that people might find them interesting and/or useful.

I have explored simplicity in many different settings: in a downtown city apartment, in suburbia, in a country cottage, in a caravan in the middle of an empty field, in an intentional community and "on the road" with a car and a tent. I have lived alone, with friends, with family – both nuclear and extended – with community members and as part of a couple. My life has seen war and peace, drought, flood, fire and earthquake. In every one of those settings, I have been both hungry and full, sick and well, happy and miserable, depressed and lively, well-off and short of cash.

My journey to simplicity has been in some ways a journey back. For my life started out in a very simple setting compared to that of my own children and grandchildren. As a child in World War Two, I found myself in a family that owned very few of the consumer goods and labour-saving devices we take for granted today. We had no refrigerator, no washing machine, no car and of course no computer or TV. Just a radio and an old, wind-up gramophone. We did not even have a telephone in the house until I was nine – the same year the war ended. There was little outside entertainment, as all lighting was blacked out and on many nights, soon after dark, the bombs would begin falling.

The images from those war years are vivid still; the tin hats, the gas masks, the thankful prayers when morning dawned and our house still stood intact, or when one of the rare letters, blue-scrawled and scissored by the army censor, came from my faraway father. Yet strangely, despite the ration books, the powdered eggs, the utterly disgusting margarine and the absence of so many things the grown-ups missed, my child's world seemed full of treats. There were sandwiches made of parsnips with artificial banana flavouring, (yes, really!) and squishy mint balls rolled in dried milk powder. We had home made Cornish pasties, deftly shaped by Grandma's expert fingers; delicious, wonderful potato cake on Sunday afternoons; saffron buns, and glasses of full-flavoured cider that came in re-usable glass bottles with pop-off stoppers that squeaked and clattered against their necks. There were flowers and home-grown vegetables in the garden, and loganberries ripened on the fence. In the nearby park was a pond, and in spring I brought home frogspawn in a jar and raised tadpoles in a shady corner by the air-raid shelter.

My grandparents, my mother and my aunts cherished and nourished me throughout those years, soothed my fears, shaped my world. And, despite the war, it was for me an amazingly good world, crammed with simple joys – Sunday dinners, country picnics, blackberry-picking expeditions, gardening, listening to the radio – where the severe scarcity of things served only to heighten our enjoyment of what we had.

I have tried, for years, to find a word that completely expresses the sweet, joyful fullness of that kind of simple, close-boundaried life, but nothing captures it. However it is that feeling, never fully named nor expressed, which has informed and shaped so many of my adult choices in later years. It is like a treasure I rediscovered and now hold close to my heart.

When I look around me now at our glutted, bored, wasteful, consumer culture, I find myself tracking back along the years, searching for the point at which the excited release from wartime privation and the welcoming back of exotic items, like oranges and bananas, real silk and coloured china, turned into insatiability: a greedy grasping for more and more and more until there seemed no boundary any longer – and nothing left to savour. (If strawberries are available year-round, where's the excitement of tasting the first one in June?) It is impossible to discern the moment when it all changed because there wasn't one. It was just a gradual, creeping change. And with that sort of change, it can take a long time before you wake up and notice what is happening.

It is said that if you try to place a frog in boiling water, it will immediately leap out, but if you place it in cold water and bring it very, very slowly to the boil it won't notice the danger until too late. And it will die. I don't know if anyone has ever literally tried this experiment – I certainly hope they have not – but you get the picture. We are all a bit like boiling frogs in this huge, consumerist, materialist, polluted pot, and we need to make our move now, before it is too late – the move to a simple, sustainable lifestyle. But how do you convince everyone of that without making it sound as though there is a lot of "giving-up" involved? People usually don't like giving things up.

However, if you pick up any one of the books on simple living – and there are quite a few of them – you will find the same theme running through all of them. It is the re-discovery of delight.

Simple living is delight-filled living. Not because we have more material things to enjoy, but because our enjoyment of the things we have increases by at least a factor of ten. Think of it this way: if you could choose between eating a huge banquet but scarcely being able to taste anything, or slowly eating one bowl of strawberries and cream with your ability to taste heightened to ten times what it is now, which would you choose?

So yes, there is some giving-up to do. But it is the giving-up of stressful lifestyles, of hyperstimulation, of addictions, of boredom, of clutter and of despair. And exchanging it for more delight. Have you heard the saying "Less is more?" Well in this case, it is. And I hope to help you prove it.

I believe that deep within many people like me – those of us over the age of forty who managed to live out most of our childhoods before the modern era of excess, of pre-packaged "infotainment," *McDonalds* on every corner, bubble-wrapped plastic toys and total *Disney*fication of the minds of children – there are intact memories of simple, home-made pleasures and the enjoyment of sufficiency. And I believe that it is up to us to mine those memories and use them to construct a better world. So in a way, I felt I had no choice but to write this book.

To me it is important that people of my age should have their say about what is happening to our world, and should put forward their ideas about what we can and should do to fix it. That is why so many of the things I have to say about the simple life are woven in with stories of my own experience. For I have lived through nearly seven decades of enormous change.

By the time my own children were born, the steady creep of consumerism was well under way. By then, I was living in a large, suburban house, surrounded by many of the modern conveniences my own childhood home had lacked. I made regular trips to the mall, and bought – within reason – whatever took my fancy. I was well and truly in the frog pot, coming slowly to the boil and not noticing it. But eventually, like many other people, I began to feel burdened by the sheer weight of my collected "stuff" and the increasing speed of my life. And around that same time, I began to realize the awful truth to which I – like most of us – had been blind for so long. Namely that for everyone in the world to live as I did, we would need at least three worlds the size of this one to sustain us all. It was a shocking realization. That was when my search for the simple life began in earnest.

I care so passionately about our beautiful Earth that I cannot bear to see it being destroyed. I know that not only our human species but the countless species of animals and plants, exquisitely evolved over billions of years, are doomed to perish if we folk in the rich countries continue to live the way we are living at present; the planet's resources cannot sustain us at this level.

So this is the second reason for writing this book. It is my way of helping to spread the word about the urgent need for cultural change and what each of us might do towards bringing that change about.

I know from my own warm memories that simple living can bring joy and contentment. But I know, also, that we cannot go back. I could not re-create, for my own children, all the details of my childhood life, even though I did incorporate as many as would fit. And neither would I want to deprive them of living fully in their own times. Life moves forward. Too often, we romanticize the past. We forget the downside of life in the old days: the fleas in the horse-hair mattresses, the unhealthy cholesterol load in the "bread and dripping", the cruelty of bear-baiting, the inhumanity of slavery, the evils of workhouse and asylum. So rather than attempting to turn back the clock, or to create some kind of anachronistic, Amish-like bubble in which to live, we need to move forward using every ounce of knowledge, wisdom, creativity and skill at our disposal to help construct a world which incorporates the best of the past with the achievements of the present and the vast potential of the future. This can be – if we do it right – a world which is based, for the first time in history, on the perfect balance and integration of the yin and the yang, the masculine and the feminine, the body, the mind, the heart, the soul and the spirit.

But each of us can only achieve this in our own lives. We cannot change the culture in which we live except – as Gandhi once suggested – by *being* the change we want to see happen. So the only sure way to go forward is to look at ourselves, at our needs, at what it is to be a human being; to work out, for ourselves, the optimum way to live, to live long, in health, harmony, and accord with other creatures in the web of life. Each of us has to be an inventor, a creator, a discoverer of the right way for humans to live. Thus each of our lives becomes a laboratory for a new experiment. Once you begin to see it this way, you realize just what an exciting project it is. And you, the reader, have already embarked on it, I know. For if you had not, you would not have picked up this book. We are pioneers together, you and I – with many, many others who are travelling in the same direction.

My search has taken me a long time. It has led me down many blind alleys. And even now, though I live a simpler style of life than many people I know, there are still things about it that I need to change. But there are some key discoveries I have made on the journey so far which I want to share with as many people as I can. Hence this little book.

Discovery – Simplicity Starts from the Inside

The first thing I have discovered about simplicity is that it grows from within, like a tree.

When I was a child, learning in Nature Study about the growth rings on a tree, I got the idea that the rings somehow got slapped on from the outside, like another layer of paint on a wall. Either I wasn't listening to the teacher (which is totally possible, as I often didn't) or no-one actually explained the process. After all, it is utterly obvious that tree growth must occur on the inside, since no-one has ever seen trees coating themselves with a new layer of bark every year, so why would anyone even need to explain it?

So of course I felt silly when I realized my error.

But that didn't stop me from making similar errors about other things, and simplicity was one of them. I really did think that simplicity came from the outside.

I saw other people shipping out their junk to charity shops and jumble sales, giving things away to friends, de-cluttering their attics and basements, and beaming with delight about how free and clear and wonderful they felt. I wanted to be like them and have that free, clear and wonderful feeling. Except that I couldn't bear to part with my junk. I wished I could give up hoarding things that "might come in useful one day". I wished I, too, could take truckloads of stuff to the tip instead of hanging on to every last button, washer, rubber band, moth-eaten jumper, birthday card, love letter, theatre programme and white elephant gift – not to mention every single one of those little black containers you get 35mm films in. And not to mention collecting even more junk because I couldn't resist wandering into every charity shop on the High Street and poring over any pile of other people's discarded junk that I happened to see, just in case, it, too, might contain something which "might come in useful one day".

I saw pictures of house interiors which were sparse and elegant, like ikebana flower arrangements, and I looked around my own cluttered house, with its photographs and calendars and books and piles of yet-to-be-filed paper and I envied those people who lived in the sparse, elegant spaces. I tried telling myself that nobody really lived like that except in magazines – until I met some people who did.

I saw and read about people cutting back their work hours, managing on less money so as to have a better family life, less stress and better health (a trend now officially called "downshifting"). And I envied them. I wished I did not have a full-time job, several part-time jobs and a hundred projects and involvements which combined to eat up every second of my time and which often plunged me into agitated states of overwhelm. I thought that if I watched and studied those people I would learn how to scale down too, and my life would be more relaxed.

(You will never believe this, I'm sure, but one of the things I was doing, in amongst all my other activities at the peak of those high-stress, busy years was teaching seminars on stress-management!)

For some reason that I never bothered to examine, I was always fascinated – right from my teenage years – by stories and books about people who went out into the depths of the countryside somewhere and bought rambling old derelict farmhouses and renovated them. I loved reading (from the comfort of my armchair, of course) about how miserable they were when they first encountered the cold, the mud, the mice galumphing up and down the insides of the walls, the weird neighbours and the sheer enormity of the task they had set themselves, and about their feeling that it had all been a terrible mistake. And how they gradually – through lots of fascinating and usually very funny (in retrospect) adventures – turned their dream into reality and lived happily ever after surrounded by quacking ducks and honking geese, new-laid eggs, sunshine and a wonderful sense of community. It always turned out that way, of course. I guess the people for whom it didn't turn out that way – and they are probably legion – are far too embarrassed to write books about how it all went wrong.

Some time around my middle thirties, I also became fascinated by the stories of people who went out (also into the depths of the countryside, usually), plonked themselves down in the middle of an empty field, or a clearing in a forest, and started creating a house out of natural materials – like mud that they sieved through an old bed-spring (old bed-springs seemed to be *de rigueur* with mud-brick builders), mixed with their hands or feet, either alone or with jolly groups of their friends who came out from the city to help and who all (of course: don't we all?) adored the idea of frolicking around making mud pies and having pasta and red wine afterwards, sitting on a straw bale.

And speaking of straw bales, there were those who had discovered you could put up an amazing and wonderful and totally eco-friendly house in a matter of days if you used straw bales – especially if you had the requisite number of those same friends who come out from the city to do this convivial stuff with the physical work and the pasta and the red wine.

Then there were those (usually the ones who chose the clearing-in-the-middle-of-a-forest option) with chainsaws, who cut down some carefully selected trees (taking care to say "Thank you") and made the most incredibly beautiful structures, usually on stilts. They were houses to die for, these. And the descriptions came complete with instructions on how to prevent termites from eating the whole thing.

The mud ones were equally beautiful, and I slavered over those.

Simplicity, I thought, came from wanting what I saw and read in those books and magazines. It came from the outside of me, like the tree slapping on its new bark.

I went to an astrologer, once. He was also a psychic, though in those days he didn't admit it. His name was Aurelio and he had a broad, beaming face, some missing teeth and a thick, Italian accent. He knew everything about me, even though he had never set eyes on me before. It was astounding. He knew about my cluttered, un-simple life. And he told me that one day I would simplify it.

I told Aurelio that I had been trying to let go of my clutter and my hoarding habits for years but that it was something I found too difficult, no matter how hard I struggled. He smiled his lovely, gappy smile and said that I should not worry about it but that one day these things would begin to fall away, all by themselves.

As he spoke, I had the image of leaves on a tree. If you try to pull them off, they resist. But when the autumn comes, one day they just let go of their own accord and flutter gently to the ground. Simplicity would be like that.

Bringing back into my life the sweet simplicity that I remembered from my childhood – a simplicity born of wartime austerity but sweetened for me by the care of a loving family who wanted all that is best for their beloved child – would not be a matter of struggling but of waiting for the signals from within. My leaves would begin to drop when my insides had changed enough to allow it. Then, and only then, would the season be right. That sounded really good.

Even so, I continued to struggle and to yearn. I, too, wanted a mud-brick house.

Introduction – Part Two
Getting Started

Let's start by asking the obvious question: what *is* a simple life?

Does the phrase immediately make you think of free-range eggs, home-grown vegetables and woodstoves? Or does it sound more like a gypsy caravan, a hippie bus or a bender in the woods?

Maybe, when you hear the phrase, you start to imagine yourself throwing out half the clutter in your attic, getting rid of one of your cars, resigning from all the committees you are on, saying "no" more often and trying to get your head (and your diary) a bit clearer. Or perhaps it conjures up dreams of selling up and buying a little, inexpensive place somewhere in Provence, or Spain, or Crete. Or is your dream to own your own island, or to restore a croft in the Highlands of Scotland?

For many people, it has connotations (perhaps slightly disturbing ones) of lowered income, since so many of the things which make our lives feel stressed and complicated have to do with the struggle to earn more money.

But for most people, it simply means to have a life in which there would be more time than there is now to spend with significant others, more time to think, dream and ponder, and more time to smell the roses. It would be a life of fewer demands, less stress and no feelings of overwhelm.

This last definition is closest to the one I had in mind when I decided to write this book. However, my definition of the simple life has four more elements to it.

The first is green-ness. By this I mean a sense that one is taking on one's share of responsibility for the future of the Earth as a living planet.

To me, this is an essential element because it gives meaning and purpose to all our efforts to simplify; a meaning and purpose which transcends our personal, individual desire to make ourselves a bit more comfortable.

The second is aliveness. By this I mean an ever-deepening awareness of ourselves as living, pulsing, sensing, experiencing creatures of exquisite sensitivity to the world around us, and a willingness to engage fully with every experience that comes along.

I believe that engaging our senses more fully enables us to move from valuing quantity to valuing quality. When our senses are fully awake and we have developed our sensitivity to stimulus in this way, we can now derive the same amount of pleasure from one perfect rose in a vase as would once have taken the entire Chelsea Flower Show to evoke. This is the key element which makes the simple life more pleasurable than any other kind of life. It is this element which brings back that delight I was talking about earlier, as in the joy of tasting the season's first strawberry.

The third element I have added is relationship. By this I mean an understanding of ourselves as parts of a whole and a sense of connection with all other humans and all other living creatures on our planet. This includes a readiness to share with them, in mutual respect, co-operation and caring.

We have all been brought up in the old, nineteenth-century worldview which saw competition between organisms (including humans) as the basic, natural law which drove evolution. This is why our economics, our politics and so much of our lives are still based so firmly on competitive models. It is only in very recent times that new discoveries in biology have revealed co-operation and symbiosis (organisms working together to mutual benefit) to be far more significant than competition.

The fourth element is spirituality. By this I don't mean religion: I mean something which is fully compatible with all religions – a sense of wonder, a sense of the sacred in all things, a humility, a reverence for the mysterious workings of a universe far too vast and immense for our finite minds to grasp. Without this spiritual element, spring is just a series of dates on the calendar, a new-born baby is just a small, damp, floppy object rather than an utter miracle, and a sunset is just a pretty picture in the sky.

My hope for this book is that it will assist you in understanding, defining, creating and maintaining thereafter exactly the sort of simple life you want for yourself. That's a big ambition, I know. But hey, why not aim high?

I hope that you will read the book slowly, try the exercises, experiment. So here we go. First, let's return to the frog pond for a few moments. Then I'll tell you about my next, big discovery. And then I'll ask you some important questions. For this book is not just about me, It is also, and most importantly, about you.

Chapter One

"Sitting Still"

How do they manage to stay so still, these frogs?

As I hold them in my torch beam, they remain motionless, unblinking. From where I stand, I am too far away to discern the telltale movements of their throats as they breathe. So for all I know, they could be small pieces of wood, carved in the shape of frogs' heads, with tiny knots in the place of eyes. Or they could be merely a trick of my own eyes, an optical illusion.

I know, though, that when they do move, it is so lightning fast that my slow eyes cannot even catch it. You have to be quick if your favourite dinner is a fast-flying insect and you have a bare millisecond in which to grab it as it whizzes by.

Evolution has given these frogs specialized cells in the retinas of their eyes which are designed to pick out movement. A frog, I have heard, can starve to death sitting on top of a pile of dead flies. You would want to shake that frog, wouldn't you? You would want to say "Look there: flies! Eat them! Don't be so *stupid*!"

And here am I, with my clever, convoluted brain, every bit as much a child of evolution as these frogs. Yet I, too, could starve to death in the midst of plenty if I did not recognize what I am sitting on as an alternative source of nourishment. Evolution encouraged me to make tools, to speak, to explore and to create. It has programmed me to search and to seek, to learn and to grow. But if I and all my people, in our search for knowledge and our love of acquiring new things, and our clever use of tools, have come to the point where that very tendency is beginning to endanger our lives, we are in big trouble. What if we are so busy watching for the next bit of amazing technology to come whizzing by and rescue us from our predicament that we fail to recognize that we are sitting on a pile of simple treasure? Then we shall perish, taking the poor frogs with us.

These frogs in my pond are so still, so quiet. I envy them their stillness, their quietness, their patience. I want more of that for myself. Since I have come to live here, I notice that I am appreciating silence and stillness more and more. The dark peacefulness of the nights is so soothing and refreshing. And in that night stillness, I can hear wonderful sounds. The wheezy bark of a fox, several fields away, the low calling of an owl, a cricket's chirp. And the sound of the breeze stirring the leaves of the hawthorn tree outside my window.

There is a small toad at the base of that tree tonight, and I just miss stepping on him (or her) as I make my way back to the house after slug patrol. The toad is probably on slug patrol too. I like toads as much as I like their cousins, the frogs. When I dug the pond, I made it as deep as I could and at the bottom I placed some old flowerpots on their sides, weighted with stones. I know that toads like such places to hibernate. Maybe this toad will spend next winter in my pond. I would like that. I pick the little creature up and carry it, cool and heavy in my hand, to the safety of a nearby flower bed, speaking my gratitude for all the slugs it has already caught and my hope for much future success in the slug hunt. The toad, dark as night, sidles away under the nasturtiums. The sweet peas nearby fill my nostrils with delight, and I pause in the doorway to take another sniff. For smells, too, are enhanced by the stillness of night. And if I didn't come out after dark, with my torch, to pick the slugs and snails off the vegetables, I would miss an opportunity to thrill my senses with these wondrous night scents.

Once, when I lived in the tropics, there was a small gardenia bush which grew right outside my bedroom window. Its scent was so heavy and so luscious that it almost kept me awake. In its branches lived a bright green tree frog which chirped all night in the same spot, catching night-flying moths and other winged things which flitted around the house, attracted by the dim light on the porch. Looking back, I think frogs have always been around, calling to me to notice them. I am glad I am noticing now and listening to their small, quiet messages. They have lots to teach me.

Discovery – The Great Paradox of Simplicity

The second discovery I want to share with you is the one I made when I began reflecting on this simplicity thing and analysing what it is all about.

It was the discovery that when you actually stop to think about it, simplicity is far from being a simple subject. In fact, as I set out on my journey to explore exactly what *is* "the simple life," the first thing I met, sitting like a boulder in the middle of the road, was a huge paradox.

It dawned on me that if you look at the average person in an average house in an average town or village in the Western world, living an average sort of life, you realize that the life he or she lives is quite complex. There are bills to be paid, timelines to be adhered to, obligations to meet, money to earn, taxes to figure out, cars to drive, a household to maintain, and a lawn to mow. There are washing machines that break down, kids who get sick, marriages that go on the rocks, tyres that go flat, and fleas on the cat. Dealing with the demands of an ordinary life is no simple matter. Which, I suppose, is why so many people dream of escaping to something simpler, more basic, more peaceful. A little cottage in the country, perhaps. Or even something on a Greek island, far away from traffic and pollution and the relentless nine-to-five slog and the twice-daily commute with all the other wage slaves.

But when you look more closely, you find that, in fact, the average life that I just described is, in many ways, the simpler option. Just as you can drive your car through traffic without spending much mental energy on what your hands and feet are doing, so can you live that average sort of life without having to think for yourself a whole lot. At the supermarket you can buy prepared meals to heat up in the microwave. Insurance – for yourself, your house, your health, your pets, your possessions – takes care of the worry about unexpected expenses that may arise from catastrophe. TV provides your entertainment, newspapers keep you informed. The school educates your children and your favourite mechanic looks after your car, which has cruise control for long drives. Your bills go on direct debit, your employer pays your salary straight into your bank, and your money is available at the touch of an ATM. Labour-saving devices do your housework, central heating keeps you warm and double glazing keeps out the noise. And when it is holiday time, a travel agent will find you a package tour that includes everything, so all you have to do is lie on the beach and turn pink.

Holidays, in fact, are a good example of the paradox. Ask people to describe what would be the most simple, basic, no-frills holiday they can think of, and they will probably say a camping trip. Yet if you have ever planned and organized a camping trip you will know that a package tour to Spain (or even Africa) is really a much simpler option, at least for you, if not for the folks who set it up for you.

So "The Simple Life," as most people imagine it, is not necessarily less trouble to live, or less trouble to organize. In fact it will probably take more planning, more thinking about and quite a lot more effort to live than the average, mainstream sort of lifestyle that most people have, in the same way that choosing dinner from the "à la carte" menu takes more energy and forethought than saying "I'll have the set meal, please."

There is really no difference between the package tour and the camping trip, because in each case someone has to organize it all. It is just that with the package tour, that part is hidden. From your point of view, it is a question of pay your money, collect your vouchers, tie on your luggage labels and go.

In the same way, the ready-to-eat meal you buy in the supermarket has been cooked and assembled by someone, somewhere, albeit on factory scale rather than in a home kitchen. What is hidden from you is not only those people's labour but the labour of the people who made the plastic container it comes in, the labour of the people who made the plastic that the container is made of, the lorry that transported both the food and the containers to the factory and then

the completed dish from factory to supermarket. And then there is
the labour of the people who made the lorry and all its components
and the people who dug the oil wells to get the oil that made the
petrol for the lorry (and the plastic for the container)... And on and
on it goes, like "The house that Jack built." All that complexity is
totally hidden from us. The simplicity of being able to buy that meal
and heat it up is paid for, if you like, by the huge but hidden complexity of that meal's creation. So if we seek that other kind of simplicity – the simplicity of the camping trip, the home made bread
and home grown vegetables from the garden – we have to take most
of that complexity back on to ourselves.

In the same way that the complexity that goes into creating the
supermarket meal is hidden from us, so is the true cost. Hidden
away out of sight in a supermarket banana, a bag of coffee beans or
a cheap shirt is the cost of the fuel it took to get them all there and
the cost in human misery and poverty experienced by growers in
far-off lands who get paid a pittance for their produce, and the
workers who toil in sweatshops or get sick and die from pesticides
in plantations and cotton fields.

So what I have realized (not in one, glorious "aha" moment but
over a number of years of exploring all this), is that if I want to live
in a way that removes me from the guilt of supporting all that, then
my life is destined to become, in certain ways, more complex, rather
than more simple. The Way of Least Resistance is the way that *feels*
simple. The Way of Consciousness, followed by most of the people
whose lifestyles we admire as "simple," does not always feel as simple on the inside as it looks on the outside. That is the paradox I discovered.

Step 1
Catching the bug

As we start out along this path I need to reassure you that simplifying is not a hardship, just in case that is how you have thought of it. It is quite the opposite. I hope you will discover, as I have, that it is one of the happiest, most rewarding, delightful and satisfying things you can possibly do.

Once that happens, you will have caught the "simplicity bug." And once you have caught that bug, the rest just follows naturally.

Another reassurance I need to make, so as not to scare you off, is to promise not to numb your mind with long tales about those planetary "herons" – pollution, global warming, the destruction of rainforests, the wanton wastefulness of our consumer society or the headlong race to self-destruction that our species seems to be engaged in. I am going to assume that you know all that stuff. If you are anything like me, your insides would scream if you thought you were going to have to listen to that again. Being forced to dwell on the awfulness of all that, once you already know about it, and already care deeply about it, is a form of torture that many "green" authors use and I hate it. It is the sort of torture that makes you want to run screaming to the bookstore for the latest blockbuster novel so that you can escape into a different world for a while and not have to think about it. Or to turn on the TV or get drunk or stoned. So there will be no litany of misery, I promise. For I know that people on the simplicity path are often highly sensitive people. Because of their sensitivity, they identify so closely with the Earth's pain that hearing about it again doesn't stimulate them to action: it numbs them. And that's the last thing I want you to do: go numb.

Furthermore, I am going to assume that you would have ignored this book altogether if you were not one of those millions of people (and we *are* in the millions) who want to do something about the solution rather than wittering endlessly about the problem. You are aware that the problem is urgent and you probably are doing something about it already (lots, maybe) but perhaps you want to do even more. And you know that we all need to live more simply so that, as Gandhi said, "others may simply live".

However, there are as many ways of doing that as there are people doing it or wanting to do it. And it is important to do it in a way that suits you, personally, rather than taking some off-the-peg version and wondering, later, why it doesn't really fit you. The aim of this book is to help you clarify your unique path to the simple life.

There are many types of "simplifiers." I have made a list of ten basic types that I have noticed, though I am sure there are more. And many of these probably overlap. We shall look, in a minute, at these different types, but first, let's start looking at you and whether you feel your own life might be improved by further simplifying it in some way.

Once we have caught the simplicity bug, and decided to make some lifestyle changes, the next thing we need to do is to qualify that. It is easy enough to say "I want a simpler life than the one I have now." But what does that actually *mean*? I am now going to invite you to give yourself ten minutes or so to sit quietly with that question. Listen to whatever inner voices you can hear and note what they are saying. Feel into it. This is the first of a number of exercises we shall do together.

> *Sit or lie quietly somewhere and think about simplicity and what it means to you.*
>
> *How would you like your life to be? How would your ideal "simple life" feel? How would it look? Take a while to imagine, to visualize, to feel into your life as you would really like it to be. Set up your ideal life, as though you were creating a new movie.*
>
> *How would that differ from what you have now?*
>
> *What would you gain?*
>
> *What would you lose?*
>
> *Don't try to come up with neat, orderly answers (unless you are the sort of neat, orderly person who simply cannot help making everything you do neat and orderly) Just let your mind free-wheel. Let it rove over the surface of the questions and simply notice what it comes up with, no matter how irrelevant (or impossible) that might seem to be right now.*
>
> *After you have pondered those questions for a while, you might care to make a note of your answers. We shall look at them again, a number of times, adding to them, amending them, clarifying them. So put them away somewhere safe.*

In the light of those answers, let us look at what sort of a simplifier you might be. Here's the list of types that I came up with, though I am sure it is by no means complete. You could probably think of others.

1. The Frugallers: Many of these have no choice. They are people who simplify their lives because they want to – or are forced to – manage on a very low income.

2. The De-clutterers: They are the ones who have finally run out of places to put things and are starting to feel overwhelmed by the sheer volume of "stuff" they have amassed. They intuitively know that by getting rid of a lot of material things, their minds will feel lighter and freer also. And that is certainly right – they will.

3. The Romantics: Romantics dream of building their own strawbale houses, keeping a house cow, growing herbs and living the "Good Life" somewhere in the country.

4. The Light Greenies: People who feel guilty that they don't try harder to follow the "3 Rs" (re-use/repair/recycle), so want to be a bit more green than they are now.

5. The Deep Greenies: Devotees of Deep Ecology who believe that all life forms have intrinsic value and that our culture is far too focused on the needs of humans.

6. The Spiritual Seekers: People who want to deepen their spiritual connection with the rest of creation by living more simply and stripping their lives of everything that detracts from their spiritual objectives, such as money, possessions, etc.

7. The Retreaters: The highly sensitive people who feel overwhelmed by the pace of modern life and want peace, solitude and a feeling of "getting away from it all."

8. The Patients: Ones who have had a "wake-up call" in the form of a heart attack or other medical crisis which served as a warning to slow down the pace of life. People with severe allergies come into this category too.

9. The Downshifters: Usually "successful" mainstream people who retire early, take redundancy or just resign, and scale down to a simpler, less stressful lifestyle.

10. The Localizers: Opponents of commercial globalization who believe that the only solution is to withdraw their patronage of global corporations and live simply within their own, local economies, leaving as light as possible a footprint on the Earth.

Can you see yourself anywhere in that list or around the edges of it? I am – or have been – in at least eight of those categories myself. As I said, they usually overlap. But knowing what sort of a simplifier you are – and what other types there are as well – can help to focus your intent as we start on our journey. And it can help you to pick out the parts of this book which are the most useful to you, as not everything will be equally relevant to everyone.

If you did not recognize your "type" in that list, then I would love it if you could jot down a new one that seems to fit you. I am sure there are other categories I have overlooked in my eagerness to produce a nice, tidy number like ten. So if yours is not there, please write it in. And let me know, so I can update the list.

Even if we feel no strong inner urge to simplify, most of us are aware that there is a need to, firstly because the way things are at the moment, the world's resources are very lopsidedly used. Some people in the world eat five meals a day and others go for five days without a meal. More than half of all the men, women and children in the USA are either clinically obese or at least seriously over-weight now, and here in the UK we are following a similar pattern. Meanwhile, six million people elsewhere are dying of starvation. I'm sure you already know that and feel concerned about it.

Secondly, there are so many of us in the world that the planet itself cannot sustain us much longer if those of us in the richer areas continue to live the way we are at the moment. And you know that too.

But men and women who work in places like Africa and India, amongst people who have nothing, discover, often to their surprise, that those people still manage to have fun and be happy a lot of the time. And, as we know, a lot of folk in our own countries who are well off , or even filthy rich, can still be miserable and stressed. So evening things up – simplifying our own lives and using up a bit less, so that others can have a bit more – is not going to spoil anything in terms of happiness or life satisfaction.

Our ancient ancestors lived a much simpler life than we do, for many millions of years. For most of those years, they lived as hunter-gatherers. Depending on the land around them for their food, for their shelter, for everything, they had to stay very much in tune with it, and with all the other creatures who shared it with them. It was a hard life, but it would have had certain benefits. There were no dishes to wash or bills to pay. No shopping for shirts or hunting for parking spots. They saw the full splendour of the night sky, unspoiled by city lights, and their lungs took in pure, unpolluted air. I am not suggesting that one should romanticize the tough, short life of a hunter-gatherer. Research on skeletons shows that the life expectancy of those early humans was only about thirty years. None of us would want to swap back to that.

Yes, it may have been great to be able to wander round in the woods in summer without your clothes on. But if you knew that any moment you might run across a sabre-toothed tiger and never make it back to the cave, that could have taken the edge off your fun a little too. So let's not waste time envying the ancients.

The point I am making is not that we should create fantasies of some golden age of the past. Rather, it is that because humans existed in that state for millions of years – far, far longer than they have existed any other way – and because our modern "civilization" has only been around for such a tiny amount of time, we are all, in our genes, hunter-gatherers. Maybe in another ten million years we shall manage to evolve into creatures whose bodies and psyches have finally become adapted to spending all day in windowless factories or sitting for hours watching TV and drinking sweet, fizzy drinks and who no longer need, for their deepest wellbeing, the sight of green landscapes, the smell of damp earth, the sound of birdsong and running streams and the feel of sunshine on their skin. Our legs might even morph into wheels if we spend a few more million years driving on motorways. But at this point in our evolution, we are still hunter-gatherers in our body rhythms, in our response to seasonal cycles and deep down in our most basic, and often unconscious, needs. So a life that is simpler in some of these ways, *i.e.* a life that is more attuned to all things "natural," is a life that brings more real contentment to our innermost selves, whether we fully realize that or not. We, too, can fit into our world as neatly and comfortably as the frogs in a pond if we learn to listen within and without, the way those distant ancestors did. We have not lost the art.

So although we have all arrived here, now, on this page, by many different routes, and our desires and goals may look very different (and the order in which we make the necessary changes may vary tremendously, depending on our individual circumstances) there is a path we can tread together for a while. It is a path which will lead us, each in our own way, to our desired ends, and will bring each one of us an increasing amount of pleasure as we go along. It is a kind of treasure hunt which is based on looking inside us for the clues, instead of outside. And that is what we shall start on, in the next chapter. But first, there is something important we need to do: to park the vehicle in which we arrived at this spot. Because the chances are, the thing which brought us here, looking for ways to make our lives simpler (and, by implication, better), was a feeling of dissatisfaction with the way things are now. It was either a feeling of dissatisfaction with our personal lives and the way we are living them, or a dissatisfaction with the way humanity in general is living its life on this planet – or both.

So the first thing we need to do is to let go of all of that. That vehicle will not be coming with us. We shall park it right here…..
and proceed on foot.

Lilypad Principle 1
Everything is Perfect
Quitting the blame game (including self-blame)

The vehicle we are going to step out of, right now, is the vehicle of blame.

For the first step on the seven-step path to a simpler life is to break yourself of the habit of beating yourself up, nagging yourself, nagging others, blaming yourself, blaming others, (including your boss, your kids, multinational corporations or the Government), grumbling, or any other sorts of negative things you might have been doing because life is not as simple as you would like it to be.

When an artist wants to paint a picture, he starts, usually, with a blank canvas. When a writer begins a story, she begins with a blank sheet of paper or a blank computer screen.

In order to create the sort of simple life you want, it is important to be able to come to the project with what the Zen Buddhists call "beginner's mind": the mental equivalent of the new page.

The trouble is, it is all too easy to sabotage a new project by letting your nice, new, clean, blank sheet become contaminated by old types of thinking, old attitudes, memories, past experiences and so on.

However, the way to avoid doing that is not to try and control your thoughts nor to attempt to force yourself into new ways of thinking or new patterns of behaviour. There is a much better technique: simply to look at yourself, your individual life and the state of the world with totally new eyes, as though you were viewing the landscape through a pair of spectacles which changed the look of everything.

Because, you see, there is absolutely nothing wrong with your present life. It is exactly the way it needs to be, right in this moment.

There is nothing whatsoever wrong with the world. Everything is just as it needs to be, right in this moment. I am serious.

There are probably all kinds of reasons – most of which are hidden from our small, human, finite minds – why everything is the way it is right now. But even if there are not, and everything is totally random, it doesn't matter and the technique still works.

Assume that everything is perfect, just the way it is.

After all, you have made the best decisions you could make, at any given moment, all through your life, right? Do you doubt that? If you doubt it, it is simply because you are looking back at those former decisions with the benefit of hindsight, which as we know is usually 20/20. Right in the moment you made any one of those decisions or took any of those actions, you did the best you could *at the time*, didn't you? People always do. Never mind that later on you wished you had done something different. For if you had known of a better way, back then, you would obviously have taken it.

If this is true for you, it is also true for everybody else in the world.

This is so simple and so utterly logical, and yet so few people seem to accept the truth of it.

One teacher I did a course with many, many years ago had a wonderful saying, which has stuck with me ever since: "There are no mistakes: only outcomes." And it is true. The concept of a "mistake" is flawed. You only recognize a mistake with hindsight. But, by definition, hindsight doesn't happen till afterwards. No-one deliberately makes a mistake, for if they did, how could it be a "mistake"?

So if you have made the best decisions you could at any given choice-point and taken the best action you knew how to take at any given moment in your life, and if everybody else has done the same, then there is no-one to blame, no-one to nag, no-one to get mad at or grumble at. Including yourself.

The world is perfect, just as it is, in this moment. OK?

Like a kaleidoscope pattern, it keeps changing. But it remains perfect.

Remember: *There are no mistakes: only outcomes.*

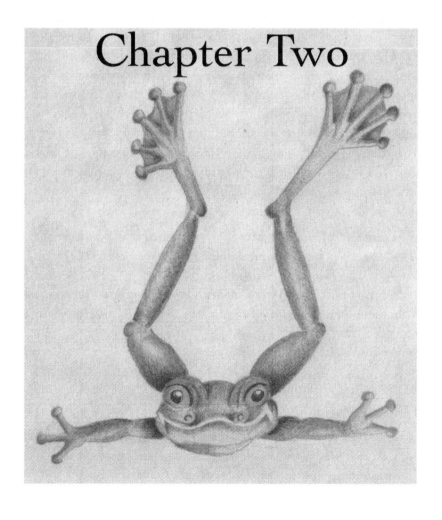

Chapter Two

"Taking the Plunge"

It is morning, and I am squatting by the side of the pond, peering in to see if the frogs are still there.

I think I have missed them though. I might have caught sight of one had I walked up the path a little more stealthily but, as always, I was too eager. And even as my eyes began to scan the pond's edges, I heard the telltale "plop" of a small body plunging out of sight. There are tiny ripples moving the patches of duckweed, but ever so slightly. These frogs take up so little room, have so little impact on their dwelling place. I try to be like that too, but it's hard. I wish everybody else would try as hard as I try. But it is not my role to judge other people or tell them what to do. All I can do is try my best to follow Gandhi's motto: *"Be the change you want to see happen in the world."* I remind myself, for the tenth time today, that everything is OK just the way it is. Finally, I relax.

It feels so peaceful up here, in the sun.

The distance from here to the far side of the pond, where the wild strawberries have claimed their territory, is only six feet. Yet as I gaze at it now, with sun shining on the water, it seems to shimmer and stretch. Through my half-closed eyes, the golden rocks darken into the pale, brick colour of clay earth, and the tall cluster of nettles beyond the far bank, by some mysterious alchemy of the mind, dissolves into a stand of eucalyptus.

How often I squatted, just as I am squatting now, gazing out across the water, watching the level falling day by day and inch by inch, and scanning the vast, Australian sky in hope of a rain cloud.

Unlike this tiny pond, which I dug by hand in one sweaty afternoon, that one – several hundred times its size – was created with a bulldozer and its bottom sealed with clay. For a while it lay bare, like a new wound, a wide, gaping hole, criss-crossed with the ribbed tracks of that great, yellow machine which had lumbered back and forth, digging and gouging, for almost an entire day. I had watched, part appalled by the ferocity of the attack and yet part fascinated by the skill of the farmer, for whom that huge thing laboured like an obedient slave, responsive to every order.

When the rains finally came, the dam filled, right to the top, and water spilled into the overflow channel, creating a tiny stream which flowed non-stop for two days. But after that, it never flowed again.

I swam in the dam that first summer, when it was full. Sure, the water was the colour of milky coffee and the oozy, slimy mud on the bottom felt unpleasant to toes more accustomed to sea sand. Under a fiery sun, the water in the top nine inches was as warm as bath water, while the layers below, where the sun's rays could not penetrate because of all the clay particles suspended in the water, were surprisingly and rather horribly cold. And I feared there may be leeches lurking under there too. Leeches terrify me.

But it was a baptism of sorts. An initiation into the life of the Australian bush; a merging of my pale, vulnerable, naked body with the fierce elements of earth, air, fire and water, and the memory of it remains strong and vivid. It was something I needed to do, just once, even if I never entered that water again. It never occurred to me, then, that the opportunity to do it again would never return.

If I could shrink, like Alice, to the size of a frog, I could slide down through the water parsnips right now and head out for the opposite shore of my little pond to rest, panting, in the shade of the nettles. But I am so big that even now, only two hours from midday on this late spring day, my shadow reaches clear across the pond. There can never be a baptism of immersion for me here. I can never know this pond with all my senses, the way the frogs know it. I can only observe it, and them, with my eyes and ears and nose, dabble my fingers in the water and perhaps use my imagination to fill in the gaps. I can never truly know this tiny world of theirs. All I can do is watch, listen and wonder – and learn.

Discovery – You Can Live Simply Anywhere

Like so many other starry-eyed innocents, dreaming of a simple life, my partner and I bought our little parcel of land in the Australian "bush" and scribbled plans for low-impact houses on the backs of envelopes. We read books and magazines that tell you how to build a house for practically nothing out of all sorts of different materials: stone, mud and straw bales, whole logs and half-logs, even old tyres. We learned how to make windows out of wine bottles, how to re-line old water tanks and how to seal a mud floor with ox blood. (First, catch your ox.) We haunted house-wreckers' yards for old doors and windows, took a course in drystone walling, and read everything we could find on the subject of mud-brick making. I even took a class in leadlighting and made a small, leadlight window. I was so proud of that window, even though I had as yet no wall to put it in.

To our friends in the city, we were pioneers. They envied our courage, admired our vision – and probably thought we were stark, raving mad.

In the summer, they came there to camp, ecstatic about our clean air, our starry nights and our peaceful life, and enjoying (or so they said) the novelty of our composting toilet and rustic, outdoor shower. We plied them with fresh, home-grown fruit and vegetables and proudly showed them the irrigation system we had constructed to bring water from the dam down to our newly-created garden and orchard.

Looking back at those years, I smile at our naivety. Some of the hundreds of trees we planted, the eucalyptus and acacias indigenous to the area, did manage to survive the punishing years of drought which followed. But most of the fruit trees perished, in the end, as year after year the rains did not come and the ground slowly dried out. Our dream of a lush oasis revealed itself for what it was – a dream. A dream in the minds of an English woman and an American man, neither of whom had any idea of the true realities of the Australian bush.

The Australian aborigines, who had lived on that continent for fifty thousand years before the white people came, knew how to watch and listen and blend in. They learned the ways of the land and adapted their lives to suit it. The Europeans tried to bring Europe with them. They tried to force the land to adapt to ideas and methods developed half a world away, where the rains came often and the topsoil was thick and rich. The Australian topsoil was thin and fragile and the weather was harsh. History tells us of all the mistakes those early settlers made. Yet the same mistakes are still being made. And our mistake was just one of those many.

Yet it was a wonderful experience: carving a homestead out of what had been thirty acres of dry grass, scrubby trees and brambles. Building a mud-brick house with my own hands is something I would hate to have missed. And living close to Nature as we did there, with kangaroos chomping grass all night within three feet of our bed, the kookaburra's raucous call waking us at dawn, lizards scuttling around our feet (not to mention the ominous presence of the brown snake who lived under our floor), was an unforgettable blessing.

But if we thought we were doing something for the Earth by our "simple living" experiment, we were kidding ourselves. Even though the house we eventually built was made of mud from its own excavation site, many of the things we brought in came from hundreds of miles away. If you add up all the energy and resources that went into creating that homestead, like the yards and yards of irrigation pipe, solar panels, batteries, inverters, pumps, water tanks, generator – the list is endless – you realize that we took from the Earth far more than we gave back in the form of a few hundred newly-planted trees and a patch of improved soil.

In the city, we had been living in a small, 150-year old, terraced house from which we could walk, cycle or take public transport to anywhere we wanted to go, so did not need a car. Being old and in a terrace, the house stayed warm in winter and cool in summer with the minimum of fuel. I haven't worked out the exact mathematics of it, but I am absolutely certain that if we had been able to measure it we would have found that our "ecological footprint" back there in the city was substantially smaller than during those years of so-called "simple living" in the bush.

I would not change it, nonetheless. For every experience of our lives holds its own particular treasure, and that one was full of lessons and insights and discoveries for me that I could probably never have gained in any other way.

The biggest discovery of them all was my realization that "the simple life" does not have to be lived in the outback of Australia or, indeed, the outback of anywhere. It can just as easily be lived in the city as in the country. You can live simply in a suburban house, an urban apartment, on a houseboat, in a guesthouse, or anywhere you choose to live. It seems so obvious now, looking back, that I am embarrassed at my own ignorance. But as I said before, hindsight is always 20/20.

Like so many people, when we thought about escaping from the "rat-race" and living more simply, we started our planning and decision-making at the wrong end. We should have done what a certain clever Swedish doctor called Karl-Henrik Robèrt did. And it is Karl-Henrik and his ideas that I am going to talk about next, for they give us a way of looking at our subject that I think you will find very useful.

Step 2
Getting Out of the Branches

Like most new projects, creating a simpler life for yourself will probably – as it most certainly has for me – bring you face to face with that old friend, the Learning Curve.

It's a bit like driving a car. It looks so simple; release the clutch and press the accelerator at the same time, and steer wherever you want to go, right? For most of us, that first driving lesson comes as a shock. Learning the feel of the gears, doing corners, hill starts, parking, watching the traffic, memorizing the rules, synchronizing all of that whilst at the same time remembering to check your rearview mirror, and avoiding pedestrians, dogs, and small kids on bikes... it all seems suddenly complex.

Once you master it, you feel smug, until your first near-miss or, worse still, accident. After which you move into a deeper level of awareness. Then there's your first skid on that icy road, and the visceral learning which that scary moment brings and for which no book learning can substitute.

Eventually, as you come close to the top of that learning curve, you have not only acquired information and developed certain skills, you have entered a new way of being. You have created such a deep relationship with your vehicle that when you are behind the wheel it feels as though you and the car are one. You sense the state of its engine, feel the tiniest change in its performance and understand its preferences.

It is ironic, isn't it, that many of us who have become so attuned to the wellbeing of our cars are using them in ways that blind us to the wellbeing of that far more essential vehicle in which we move and live: the body. We deprive our bodies of exercise by driving to places where we could easily walk and use them to increase the stress that makes us ill: zooming along motorways at speeds that our bodies were never meant to experience, breathing in fumes, sitting tensely in traffic jams, bombarding ourselves with ionised air particles that sap our energy and give us headaches... and on and on.

Furthermore, although we now possess, collectively, a stack of knowledge and understanding about the ways in which the Earth's ecosystems sustain themselves and the conditions which are necessary for the healthy functioning of this little, blue planet we call home, and all the forms of life which are part of it, humans are steadily wrecking the whole thing. And that is more than ironic; it is an insane tragedy.

It is becoming increasingly obvious that if human beings – particularly those in the affluent, Western, industrialized countries who are mainly responsible for the twin problems of over-consumption and pollution – don't learn new ways of being, and start adopting them now, most forms of life on Earth will come to an end. To get from where we are now to where we need to be for our lives to be sustainable, we as a race are facing the steepest learning curve ever. People are standing around shaking their heads. Where to begin?

The place to begin, for each of us, is with ourselves. And the way to begin is to go all the way back to basics in our thinking. What are the essential conditions which must be met if we are to live sustainably?

A Swedish oncologist called Karl-Henrik Robèrt faced this very same question back in the 1980s. Karl-Henrik was an expert on cells. He spent much of his professional life peering into microscopes and he knew all about malignancies – how cancer cells, spreading out of control, finally kill their host. He was also a lover of the natural world, and a father. As he watched his children growing up, he felt increasingly concerned about ecological issues.

Karl-Henrik knew that the cell, whether of animal or plant, is the basic unit out of which every living thing is composed and that cells have certain requirements which must be met if life is to continue. As he said in his autobiographical book, *The Natural Step*:

"We cannot discuss politics or ideologies with cells; they are only concerned with the conditions necessary for sustaining and propagating life. They also remind us that we are inescapably a part of nature."

As he pointed out, you need to go right down to the molecular level to discern any difference between the cells of a human being and those of a seal or an eagle. And even at that molecular level, our genes are 98% identical to those of chimpanzees. So what is good for a living cell is good for us (and for all life on our planet) and what is bad for a cell spells trouble for all of us and for our entire world.

"It was clear," Karl-Henrik said,"..that if the prerequisites of cells were not met, species would go, and the most advanced ones – the newcomers in evolution that are the most complex and vulnerable – would suffer the greatest losses. If pollution and deterioration of our habitat continued, the endpoint would be a republic of grass, microbes and insects."

With this thought, he had reduced the multitude of environmental problems that he saw around him to one, basic, underlying principle – whatever keeps healthy cells healthy is good: whatever damages healthy cells is bad.

He had an overwhelming urge to tell everyone he knew about these insights. He imagined himself racing into a radio station, grabbing the microphone from the startled announcer and screaming out his truth to the whole nation. Instead, he collected around him a group of eminent scientists, experts in a number of different fields, and together they hammered out a document which set out the basic, scientific, fundamental conditions essential to the health of living cells. He then, with the support of his Government and the King of Sweden, raised enough money to mail out a pamphlet about it to every household in the country. From there, he went on to create The Natural Step movement, which is aimed at persuading companies (particularly manufacturing companies) to green up their methods by going back to basics and, from there, working out the details of how and how soon they may be able to effect the necessary changes. (One of the first to take The Natural Step was the furniture manufacturer, IKEA, and many other high-profile companies have followed.)

Anyway, back to Karl-Henrik. When it came time to present his ideas to others, the metaphor which came to him was that of a tree.

Basic principles – the requirements for the healthy functioning of living cells – form the trunk of a tree. As you apply these principles to all the aspects of your life, you find yourself moving out along the various branches; physical health, mental health, emotional health, public health, health of the soil, the forests, etc... all these are branches off the main trunk. Each of these can be followed to its smaller branches. The branch called "physical health," for example, leads to things like healthy lungs, healthy heart, healthy teeth. From there you get to the twigs: quitting smoking, getting more exercise, flossing... From these twigs hang your individual decisions, such as "From now on, I'm going to drink two litres of pure water a day... I'll take a brisk, two-mile walk each morning... must buy myself a better toothbrush... switch to eating organic vegetables... " Those are the leaves.

To me, this is a wonderful basis for decision-making. It is all too easy to get lost in the leaves, but if you go to the trunk first and then move slowly up a branch, everything is much clearer. Likewise, if you find yourself thinking about a particular leaf, trace it back till you can identify the branch from which it sprang, and it will have a lot more meaning for you. (Flossing your teeth might just seem like an annoying chore, if seen in isolation, but in fact if practised regularly it improves oral health which, in its turn, improves your ability to fight infection, thereby leading to better overall health and vitality and a more efficient functioning of all your cells.)

This tree principle gives us an excellent way of approaching the issue of simplicity. Many of us, when we get in touch with the desire for a simpler life, dive straight into a pile of leaves instead of sitting down and analyzing exactly what it is about our lives that we want to simplify.

In his book, *Simplicity and Success*, Bruce Elkin, who describes himself as a "Personal, Professional and Executive Coach" for people wanting to simplify their lives, gives some examples of this. Many would-be simplifiers, he says, instead of thinking it through carefully, rush into a drastically pared-down lifestyle, only to find that later, when the novelty wears off, it is not as satisfying as they hoped it would be. This is usually because (a) they have focused on the negatives (the things they didn't want in their lives) instead of the positives (the sort of life they wanted for themselves) and (b) they had failed to look deeply at their own needs, the things and activities which gave them pleasure and satisfaction, and so had thrown some of these out in a zealous burst of self-sacrifice.

Elkin cites the example of one couple who, for budgetary reasons, decided that they could no longer afford to buy any books. Yet reading had always been one of the chief pleasures of their lives. If they had planned their simplifying properly, books would have been the last thing to come under the knife.

Yes, for sure, if we downshift in our income we shall need to make budget cuts. But let's be skilful about this and not cut the very things which give our life its greatest pleasure and meaning. Let us look at how we can bring more pleasure and joy into our lives, not less. Please, if you remember nothing else about this book you are reading, remember this:

Simplicity is not – and never should be – a hair shirt.
It is merely the embrace of a new kind of joy.

If you were the argumentative type, you might now turn round and ask me, "But what if 'the very things which give my life its greatest pleasure and meaning' are getting drunk, snorting cocaine, binge eating, going on shopping sprees, driving round in a petrol-guzzling SUV and having three more cars at home in the garage?"

Well for a start, if all that were true, you probably wouldn't be reading this book. But let's take the question seriously, using the same tree metaphor. Drinking to excess, taking drugs, shopping sprees and status cars are all twigs and leaves of another kind of tree. If we were to trace the drunkenness back to its main branch, we would probably find something other than pleasure there – most probably an escape from emotional pain, a need to 'belong' or a physical addiction to alcohol. The urge to shop, likewise, can have similar origins, as in the popular expression "retail therapy".

Much addiction, particularly to alcohol, begins with an attempt to self-medicate for depression, and shopping often serves the same purpose. So does binge eating. The desire for large, powerful cars often grows out of feelings of personal inadequacy or a fear of sexual impotence, and the resulting need to impress others and shore up our own self-esteem. So while we imagine that these things bring us pleasure, what they actually bring us (or what we hope they will bring us) is not so much pleasure as the cessation of an inner pain or longing of some kind. They are ways to fill a kind of hole inside us. (I shall be talking more, later, about this hole, for getting to know what our individual holes might be is one of our key steps to the simple life.)

I used to face similar questions regularly as a health educator when I was giving talks on nutrition. If we rely on our feelings to tell us what is good for us, how do we distinguish between healthy things, like an organically-grown apple, and a glass of Coca-Cola or a cup of coffee?

To me, the answer is simple. Wait a few hours and check again. Does your body remain grateful? Whilst the pleasure of crunching your way through the juicy apple, sipping the sweet drink or feeling the hit of the caffeine in the coffee might be hard to tell apart, anything which is addictive (and that includes sugar and caffeine) will first take you up and then bring you down. The apple, on the other hand, will have no side-effects.

Although our efforts to fill our inner, unfillable holes may succeed in the short term (just as the glass of Coke feels good in the short-term) in the long term it just doesn't work. The sense of emptiness – or inadequacy or desire for more booze, more drugs and more shopping – *always* comes back.

So this crucial second step in our quest for a simpler life has nothing to do with budgeting, with moving to the country, building a straw bale house, home-schooling our kids or swapping our Aston-Martin for a bicycle. It doesn't even have to do with clearing out the attic and taking our cast-offs to Oxfam. It has to do with reflecting deeply on who we are and what sort of a life we would actually like for ourselves. Not what that life would look like from the outside, or how others might see it, but how it would actually *feel* to be living it.

The important thing, with this step, is to make sure you stay out of the branches. Get right down to the roots and trunk of who you are and what are the basic conditions which would enable you to live a life which is simple, pleasant, enjoyable and deeply satisfying.

If you have ever studied psychology, you will probably remember Abraham Maslow's famous pyramid. He saw human needs in the form of a pyramid, with the most basic, survival needs at the bottom – oxygen, water, food, shelter, clothing, etc. For most of us in our modern society (since we cannot just go and select a cave, hunt game, skin a bear and collect nuts and berries), the need for food, shelter, clothing, etc translates into the need for a basic income with which to purchase these necessities for ourselves.

The next set of needs in the pyramid are those which have to do with our relationships with other people, such as our need to be cared for, to be liked, to be respected, admired, etc. and to feel part of something larger than ourselves – our families, our groups of friends, our tribes and societies.

As we know, the foundations of one's sense of identity as an indi-

50   The Lilypad List

vidual are formed by one's childhood. Each of us, as an impressionable, flexible and infinitely adaptable little person coming into the world, is shaped and moulded according to the family situation in which we find ourselves; by the feelings, behaviours, attitudes and practices of our parents and other caretakers; the personalities and particularities of our siblings, if we have them; and by the particular, in-house "culture" of our family home, which in turn is influenced in myriad ways by the wider culture beyond its walls.

Thousands of books have been written on this subject, but most of them boil down to the same basic set of simple facts which states that:

- Because this shaping and moulding process has so many variables in it – and because each of us comes into the world with a slightly different genetic endowment anyway – each one of us, even identical twins, is a unique organism.

- Because of that uniqueness, each of us has his or her own, particular way of getting all the needs in the pyramid filled. Though oxygen is our most basic need, even our breathing patterns can differ slightly and, from there on up the pyramid, the differences become more and more pronounced.

- Because of that uniqueness, each one of us is the ultimate expert on how we want our needs to be filled.

However:

- Because of all those variables in the developmental years, our shaping and moulding can twist us into some rather uncomfortable shapes, and one of the tasks of our adult life is to understand those uncomfortable shapes and to take remedial action where necessary, to smooth them out.

- One of the uncomfortable bits of moulding that often happens is that we develop "need-holes" in places where our childhood needs have been unmet, or less than completely met.

The more adequately we have understood, and dealt with, our need-holes, the more successful our journey to the simpler life is likely to be. Because it is more than likely that our need-holes are the underlying cause of any addictions we may have. They are the source from which many of our desires spring, even though we often don't make the connection.

The need-holes hide between the roots of the tree, and if you trace their influence all the way up, you end up in the twigs and leaves of flashy sports cars, chocolate cake, workaholic behaviour, and two-hundred-and-forty pairs of shoes (some still in their original boxes and bags).

A need-hole creates a yearning in the psyche. But who, at thirty-four or forty or fifty-two, can give voice to a need for the bliss and sweetness of drinking at a mother's breast, for the respect and patient, timeless attention of a loving father, for a fun and joyful playground free from lurking bullies, cruel taunts and relentless competition? So the unfilled needs for closeness, security, physical affection, unconditional love, patient, caring attention and a sense of achievement translate themselves into desires more age-appropriate: the chocolate cake (so blissfully sweet!), the sports car (Now you'll look at me!), the brass plate on the office door (Daddy will have to approve of me now, surely?) and so on.

The problem is, whilst you can fill a hole in the ground, you cannot fill a hole which exists only in memory – a historical hole. Trying to fill a historical hole is like trying to fill a leaking bucket.

Take a look around at all the people around you who definitely aren't living simple lives and who are definitely not happy. Observe those people on treadmills, working more and more hours and looking more and more haggard, shopping more frantically, clawing their way up status ladders, and so on. Don't they look to you suspiciously similar to a population frantically and obsessively pouring water into leaking buckets?

It is easy to see this pattern in others, especially in its more glaring manifestations. But in fact most of us (perhaps all of us) have it to some degree. And that is what this step of the journey is about: identifying your own leaky bucket, your own need-hole.

What deeper yearning lies at the roots of your tree of desire?

Lilypad Principle 2
Time Out is Essential
Giving yourself time, space and silence

In the previous chapter, I have given you (I hope) a lot to think about and feel into. And this thinking about and feeling into – especially as regards the deeper aspects, like the need-holes – cannot happen unless you make space and time in your life for a bit of healthy introspection.

Many of us (perhaps most of us in twenty-first century, Western society) keep ourselves so busy and so exposed to outside stimulus – radio, TV, CDs and videos, newspapers and magazines, e-mail, other people, traffic noise, mobile phones – that there is almost no time at all to sit quietly alone with our thoughts and feelings.

In fact, as a lifelong lover of peace, silence and solitude, I discovered to my amazement some years ago that heaps of people are terrified of silence. "If I sit in silence," one woman said, "I am frightened that I shall be swamped with fearful thoughts."

"I feel really scared," said another, when I had invited a group to spend half an hour without speaking. "I have never done anything like this before. It feels really weird and frightening."

"If I find I can't cope with it," another said, "I might just slip out of the room; is that OK?"

Yet it is only when we give ourselves time to disengage from the hubbub around us and sit quietly with our thoughts – or go for a solitary walk, bike ride or swim, and let the thoughts, ideas and feelings flow freely as we move – that we can get in touch with the deeper currents of who we are and what we really want.

For some people, writing in a journal is a good way to engage this process of self-discovery. For others, working alone in the garden, or engaging in some repetitive activity like painting a fence or knitting, alone and in silence, is preferable to sitting still. However you choose to do it, the essence is to disengage and to go within, to see what is going on beneath the surface of your everyday life.

Holidays, which were invented so that people could take time out from busy lives and relax, can often become as busy (and almost as stressful) as the workaday lives from which they were supposed to give us a break. If you doubt this, think crowded motorways, airport check-in and security queues, cramped aeroplanes, delayed trains, planes and buses, overcrowded holiday destinations, puzzling maps, sunburn, over-priced theme parks, the frustrations of making yourself understood in another language, mosquitoes, missing tent-pegs, noisy neighbours, lumpy beds, grumpy children... I don't know about you, but it takes me several days just to relax into being on holiday and catch up on sleep.

Despite all that, a holiday does refresh and invigorate me and I think that applies to most of us. We definitely need time out, every so often. But the simple life, for me, and probably for you, demands more time out than a fortnight in Spain and a couple of short breaks in the countryside. It demands that we build regular doses of time, space and solitude into our lives, year-round. It is only when we create these islands of tranquillity for ourselves that we start to appreciate and enjoy the treasures of simplicity. That is why the "slow food" movement is gaining such popularity. No-one deeply savours or enjoys a hurried meal.

So slowing down is one of the key techniques for moving to a simpler life. But it is almost as though we have to re-learn how to do it, especially since so many other people around us keep right on dashing about like grasshoppers on amphetamines.

Buddhist teacher Thich Nhat Hahn advises people to think of it this way: for optimum spiritual and emotional health – and in order to be effective in the world – time out for rest, relaxation, contemplation, meditation (or just sitting quietly, disengaged from all potential distractions), should comprise some weeks in every year, some days in every month, and some number of minutes (at least fifteen, I would suggest, and ideally more than that) in each day.

So you may like to start figuring out how you could rearrange your life to accommodate these regular periods of rest and renewal.

Right now, the second action step on this path to simplicity is to schedule some time in the next few minutes, hours, days or weeks to do the exercises suggested in this book, so that the ideas and suggestions can percolate.

By doing this, you will be customizing the programme to suit your own, unique needs and visions.

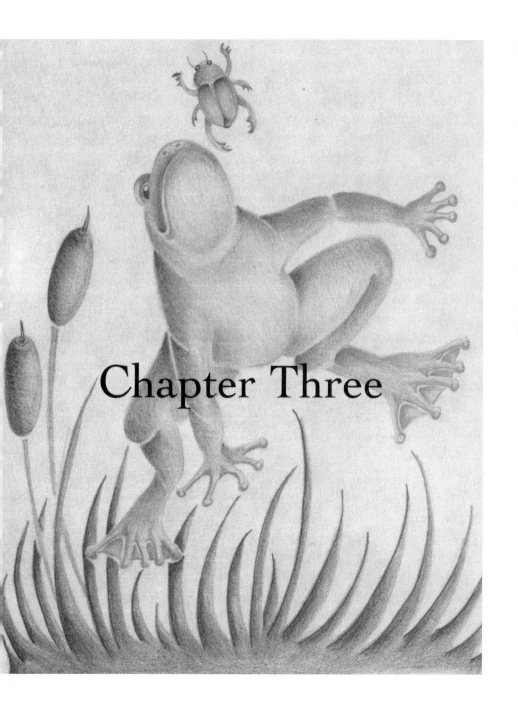

Chapter Three

"Voices from the Swamp"

The days have lengthened and the water in the pond has lost its chill. Some of the frogs are still around, but nowadays I am more likely to find them elsewhere in the garden, lurking in the cool, green spaces under carrot fronds or disappearing into the long grass at the base of the fence. Like teenagers setting off for college, they will be moving further and further afield, sampling the world, risking its dangers and learning its lessons. Many, like the flattened one I saw in the lane this morning, will not survive. Their small, purring voices will never be heard, now.

Not that they ever say much, these frogs.

They seem to be a reticent species, reluctant to give their opinions or to speak much above a whisper. The sounds around this pond are very quiet and decorous compared to other places I have been. Like a certain swamp in Louisiana, USA, where I learned another important lesson from frogs.

We camped there, not far from the edge of that swamp: a vast, wet, green tangle of lush life. The humid air was so dense with moisture that I wondered whether moss would start to grow on the backs of my hands if I stayed there too long, or ferns sprout from my ears.

But it seemed a quiet place, and we were the only campers there. We were so grateful for that. For up till then, on that camping trip, we seemed to have been pursued by noise: motorbikes, yapping dogs, blaring radios, noisy people with shrill voices and children who didn't go to bed till midnight, generators that chugged away all evening so that campers could have all the comforts of home, including television. Here, at last, it was blissfully peaceful. We fell asleep to the light, murmuring voices of frogs.

Waking part way through the night, I noticed that the music had now changed. The light, soprano frog voices had yielded to a louder, deeper chorus. Tenor and baritone frogs were filling the night air with their songs and conversations. I went happily back to sleep, cradled by this new sound.

Two hours later, I stirred again, briefly. Just long enough to notice that everything had changed once more. Now, the thunderous, bass voices of bullfrogs completely filled the night. Despite the cacophony, I slept peacefully again.

Next morning, we discussed the irony of it. One simple truth stood facing us. It is not the decibels which matter. It is our judgement about noise which makes it acceptable or not acceptable. However loud it may have been, the nocturnal choir of frogs did not bother us one bit, whereas we had found all previous campground noises stressful. It was a humbling lesson. And it taught me a lot about the real nature of stress. It's not the thing outside me that is the problem. The problem is on the inside – in the story I tell myself about it.

Discovery – The Shadow of Stress

I used to think that stress was a bad thing, to be avoided as much as possible. That was before I studied it.

When I began reading books and journal articles on the subject, I soon discovered that stress, like fire, is in itself neither good nor bad, but neutral.

Stress, in its most basic meaning, refers to some kind of pressure, strain or force. It derives from the Latin word *stringere*, meaning "to draw tight". It is the principle which enables guy ropes to keep a tent upright and that which, when you are out for your morning jog, enables the elastic to keep your sweat pants from tumbling embarrassingly around your ankles.

It can be useful at a mental level also. As a writer, I know that without the "pressure, strain and force" of a looming deadline I am far less likely to get a piece of work completed.

However, if the waistband of your sweat pants is not quite loose enough, you start feeling uncomfortable, and if the guy ropes on the tent are too tight they can pull the pegs out of the ground or tear the tent fabric. Stress has to be in the right amount to be useful but not enough to cause problems.

We all know that stress is one of the biggest underlying causes of illness in our modern world. Which means that we are, in a million different ways, subjecting ourselves to a higher-than-useful level of "pressure, strain and force".

Some of this is purely physical. We hurtle our bodies through space in cars and aeroplanes at much faster speeds than they were designed for. These bodies, shaped by millions of years of evolution to move actively through the forest – alert, attentive to every sight and sound, breathing pure air – are squashed and strapped into the confines of narrow seats, in pressurized cabins with stale, recirculating air, or in cars crackling with static electricity, sealed off from

the surrounding landscape which appears to whizz by far too quickly for the eye to attend to properly. We force ourselves to sit for long
periods, often in badly-designed chairs, in front of screens of various kinds, and put strain on our digestive organs by eating junk
food, frequently on the run.

Stress is also mental and emotional. In this case, just as in my
story of the frogs in the swamp, it is usually our good/bad judgements about things which make them stressful. A man or woman
with a happy-go-lucky temperament, who has an assignment to finish by a certain date, is likely to have the attitude that: "If it gets
done, it gets done, and if it doesn't, well that's just too bad and I'll
deal with that when the time comes." A tense, uptight person will
feel more and more worried about it, more and more under pressure
as the deadline approaches. He or she may lie awake at night, thinking:"But what if... ?" In other words, it is often the stories we tell
ourselves about the events in our lives which create stress, not the
events themselves.

Sure, there are universally stressful events: earthquakes, fire and
flood, accidents, bereavement, divorce, illness – all these place stress
on the human organism, regardless of temperament. Even happy
events like weddings and Christmas are stressful to some degree.
Nevertheless, our attitudes to these events and the stories we tell
ourselves about them can increase or decrease substantially their
level of stressfulness.

Most of us are already aware of all this.

But there is one discovery I made about stress which came as a
huge surprise to me. This is that stress has a hidden, shadow side
that is not generally talked about; like alcohol, heroin and sugar, it
can be addictive.

I discovered this many years ago, when I returned to work after
a three-month vacation.

My job at the time, in a busy, community health centre, was generally acknowledged to be a very stressful one. The resources of the
centre could only barely cope with the demand, and all staff were
working at full capacity and beyond. Before I left for that extended
vacation, I had spent several weeks working at an even faster, more

frantic pace than ever, in the effort to get all the loose ends tied up before I handed over to my locum. The last day, I worked till late in the evening. Finally, it was all done. All the obsessive, last-minute instructions I'd written on Post-It notes were stuck to the necessary documents, my desk was clean, and I left.

Three months later, after a wonderful holiday in which I had toured all around Europe, I came back into my office relaxed, refreshed, and totally free of any feeling of stress.

Within half an hour, the pace had quickened. Files and notes were landing on my desk, the phone began ringing, requests came pouring in. And as I stood there, listening to someone's voice on the phone and watching my "in" box filling up, I suddenly became aware of a strange sensation. It was as though, for the first time, I had become aware of the sound of my own inner engine. After three months of quiet idling, it was now revving back up and I could almost hear the rising sound of those revs somewhere in my solar plexus. What's more, it was accompanied by a shocking, inner pleasure. It was as though my body was saying "Wheeeeee!" like a child on a merry-go-round as the speed picked up and the horse she was sitting on began to rise through the air. It reminded me a lot of the feeling you get when you have had no tea or coffee for ages and someone hands you a cup of it and it suddenly tastes ultra-delicious: "Ahhhh, that is what I have missed."

Stress is addictive.

After that, I started noticing the tiny smirk at the edges of the faces of those colleagues who were complaining how busy they were. How busy, how important, how special, maybe even indispensable, they were. Their egos, and mine, were feeding on the stressful nature of our work. Yes, there are shadow aspects to stress.

So as we move forward in our journey to the simple life, let's pay careful attention to the inner landscape. Turn over all the stones, look for the shadow side of things. Question everything. Take nothing for granted.

Step 3
Jumping Off

As you can see, my approach to the "how" of simplifying begins not with buying a bramble-filled block of land at the end of a country lane and setting to work with a scythe and a spade – although you certainly can if you want to and the exercise will probably do you good – but with a journey inwards; a journey of self-discovery.

You'll probably find brambles aplenty there too. They will be the brambles of self-neglect, brambles of discontent, brambles of habit, brambles of addiction. I don't necessarily mean physical addiction (though you may well find some of those for at least half the population is addicted to some substance or another, the two most common being caffeine and sugar) but you are likely to find addictions of some other kind as well – to beliefs and attitudes, feelings and perhaps even outdated commitments of one sort or another, whether to people or to principles. Many of these, too, may need to be scythed and to have their stubborn roots dug out.

Way down under the brambles, there will almost certainly be need-holes. Very, very few of us are free of those.

So let's start exploring this territory a little. We'll start with the physical health aspects. For the simple life is, above all, the healthy life at all levels. (Remember Karl-Henrik's basic criterion: what is good for our cells is good for the planet.)

The body is designed to work efficiently for a goodly number of years, provided it is well-maintained, so we need to keep it in good working order. But a lot of people don't. "Self-neglect" is a harsh phrase for me to use, I know, but many of us let weeks, months and even years go by without paying full attention to our physical well-being. That is how illness happens. We forget to pay attention to the ongoing, everyday needs of our bodies for healthy food, lots of pure, filtered water, clean air, exercise (all three kinds: aerobic for our heart and lungs; stretching for our whole bodies, especially the joints; and load-bearing for our muscles) and sufficient, sound sleep.

We fuss over our cars, keep them filled with petrol, check their oil and tyres regularly and make sure the brakes don't wear too thin. At the same time, we gobble junk food, starve ourselves of sleep, and wear out our adrenal glands from too much stress. Many people take better care of their cars than they do of themselves. If their cars wear out, they can buy new ones, but it doesn't seem to occur to them that the bodies they live in are handed out at only one per person per lifetime. There are no compulsory M.O.T inspections for these most important of all vehicles.

The trouble is that unlike cars, bodies have an enormous and wonderful capacity for self-repair. So they are much easier to abuse. Treat your car badly and it will have no hesitation in conking out in the middle of the motorway, leaving you stranded and cursing. Mistreat your body, and it will still try its best again and again, like a patient, faithful donkey, to get you where you want to go. (And how often do you remember to thank it for that?)

However, when we learn to tune in deeply to our bodies and their needs, we often find that they are trying to whisper messages of distress. It pays to listen for a whisper like that, before it becomes first an audible groan, then a shout, then a scream.

Sickness, as you know, is often apparent at subtle levels before it emerges physically as full-blown disease. If we don't heed the little tap on the shoulder, (loss of energy, lifeless-looking hair, spots on the skin, tension headaches, insomnia) it becomes a dig in the ribs (migraine, irritable bowel, slipped disc) and, eventually, a hit on the head by a 2 x 4 ("Oops – what am I doing in this hospital bed?!!")

The automatic response of most people in our culture to physical pain or discomfort is to pop a pill and keep on going. Our conventional Western medicine encourages this attitude by its tendency to treat symptoms instead of root causes. Unfortunately, despite the undeniable gifts it has given to the world, medicine has also become a lucrative industry with a vested interest in having a supply of sick people to treat. So when something goes seriously wrong with us, all our so-called "health" system knows how to do is to patch us up, sell us more pills, and put us back where we were before.

The holistic practitioner, and the wise individual, know that pain and discomfort of any kind is the body's way of signalling some deeper distress or imbalance. Addressing that imbalance as early as possible, before it leads to sickness, is by far the simplest choice.

The frenetic, pressured way of life which so many people live nowadays is not a healthy one for an animal to live. But we are animals. Measured on the time scale of evolution, our emergence from the forest happened only a fraction of a second ago. So our animal bodies will guide us, more surely than anything else, to the places where simplifying is called for in our lives.

This is the "where" of simplifying. To see where we need to make the necessary adjustments, we are going to look first at our physical selves, then our mental and emotional selves.

Let's turn, then, to the messages coming from your body and the way you are living in it right now, and see if there are any indicators there. If your life is not as simple as your body needs it to be, in order to maintain optimum health for all your cells, there will almost certainly be indicators. Like little LED lights on your inner dashboard, there will be messages coming from your physical, mental, emotional or spiritual innards, warning you that change is necessary.

Here is a test which will help you to recognize some of those warning signs – signs which you either have not noticed or have noticed but are still trying to ignore. I call it the Sick Canary Test, and I am sure you can guess why I chose that name. Remember how the miners, in the old days, used to take a canary down the mine with them? If there were toxic fumes in the air down there, the canaries, being highly sensitive creatures, would keel over and die, whereupon the miners would hastily retreat from that spot.

We all have a highly sensitive pet canary. It is our physical body. If we are living the sort of life which thoroughly suits our basic, animal nature, then the canary sings contentedly. If not... *simplify*!

The Sick Canary Test

Are you splitting off from your body and its needs, cycles and rhythms? Take this test and see. (Score 3 for "Often", 2 for "sometimes", 1 for "just occasionally" and 0 for "never".)

1. Do you watch TV because you are too tired to do anything else?

2. Do you get less sleep than you really need?

3. Do you skip meals because you are too busy to stop?

4. Do you feel overwhelmed by your tasks and obligations?

5. Do you ever need a stimulant, such as coffee, to get you through?

6. Do you ever curse your natural rhythms (your menstrual cycle, your "slumpy" time of day, your energy fluctuations)?

7. Do you turn to fast food and instant meals because you are too busy to cook?

8. Do you dread mid-life, menopause, old age, baldness, turning fifty, drooping breasts?

9. Do you drive everywhere because there isn't time to walk or catch a bus?

10. Do you tend to skimp on exercise or meditation whenever something urgent needs doing?

11. Do you find yourself saying "Hurry Up!" to your partner, your kids, your friends, your dog?

12. Do you feel a pressure in your chest or gut at traffic lights, in queues, waiting for things to download on your computer?

13. Do you go for hours without laughing?

14. – or without singing?

15. – or without stretching?

16. Do you postpone going to the toilet because you are busy with something else?

17. Do you forget to drink plenty of plain, filtered water as well as other drinks ?

18. Do you suffer from tension headaches ?

19. Do you go for days without cuddling another human or other live creature ?

20. Do you spend more than two thirds of your waking hours indoors ?

Scoring: 0-10 = you're doing well; 11-20 = check your priorities; 20+ you may be a sick canary; 40+ it's time to call the vet.

How did you score?

Millions of people in our industrialized, Western culture would score somewhere between twenty and forty on this test. So if you, too, scored high, you are probably closer to our culture's "normal" than someone living a really simple, healthy life. But it is a weird sort of normality. We may appear to be fitting in to the world around us just as well as those frogs in my pond fit into theirs. If, on the inside, we are stressed out, it is likely that everyone around us is too. But it is a dangerous conformity. Since our culture has shifted the goalposts, we imagine we are normal. But the stressed-out life of a sick canary is not normal for our animal organisms at all. If we are struggling to stay ahead of our bills, struggling to "get ahead," or to keep up with a whole streetful of Joneses, our lifestyles may actually be making us sicker and sicker.

This means that each step we take towards a simpler life is probably going to take us further away from our culture's idea of normality, and we must be prepared to cope with that. There may even be opposition from other people who feel threatened in some way by the changes we make. (I'll talk more about this in Chapter Six.)

The changes are important to make, nonetheless. If we don't listen to these early warning signals, then not only are we heading for trouble in terms of our own health and mortality, we are also contributing to the troubles of the planet. What we need to fit in with is not the Jones's phoney, resource-gobbling, stress-making, consumer pond but the pond that Nature herself has created. It is the real, ever-recycling, ever-changing world of wind and weather, rock and tree, soil and water that we have to fit in with. If we don't, the herons of addiction, the herons of sickness and the herons of nervous breakdown may one day pluck us from these lives that look so normal and healthy and eat us for dinner.

Quite apart from all the environmental implications, if you scored high on the Sick Canary Test, then simplifying your life is an urgent need, *for the sake of your own health*.

However, environmental issues and health issues are inextricably connected. Ernest Callenbach speaks of what he calls "The Green Triangle." Every would-be simplifier needs to know about that triangle.

The three points of the triangle are:

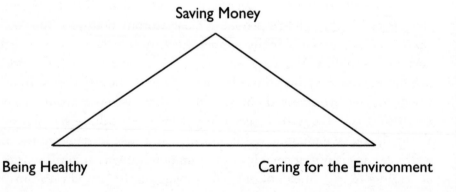

Saving Money

Being Healthy   Caring for the Environment

Callenbach points out that whenever you do something benefi-cial for one of the points on that triangle, you will almost certainly be doing something beneficial for the other two as well, whether intentionally or otherwise.

He gives the example of deciding to improve one's health, by eat-ing less fatty meat and dairy products. Not only would such a deci-sion lower one's chance of circulatory disease, and have a number of other health benefits as well, it would also save money, since meat and dairy products are relatively expensive items. Furthermore, such a decision would benefit the environment too. Meat produc-tion is one of the most wasteful uses of agricultural land and there-fore takes up farm resources that could be better used in other ways.

He goes on to explain that you can start at any point of the tri-angle and get the same result. When you do something beneficial for the environment, like walking or bicycling instead of driving, you are helping to cut down pollution emissions, to reduce smog and lung damage, and to decrease acid rain. But at the same time you are creating a benefit for your own health, since you will get more exer-cise. And of course by leaving your car at home you will save a lot of money on petrol, oil and car repairs.

Whenever you save money by avoiding the purchase of all unnecessary consumer items, you will also be saving that little bit of the Earth's resources which would go into the manufacture of those items. And when you are not buying "stuff," you need less money. That of course means you do not have to work so hard to earn it, which means more leisure time, more time to spend with those you love, or in creative pursuits or in quiet reflection – or simply in hav-ing fun. All of which can lead to a higher level of mental, emotional – and therefore physical – health.

So look again at your score on the Sick Canary Test. If it is greater than ten, make a note of which are the most important things which will need to change if that score is to be reduced. And remember that whatever you change to reduce that score, you will be doing something not only for yourself but for the planet also. (And, as Callenbach explains, you'll probably be saving money at the same time.)

You might like to revisit, now, those notes you made at the beginning – about the sort of simple life you would like to be living – and to add in something about how that life might be if you were to make the changes indicated by your Sick Canary score.

Let's take a few moments here to look again at the issue of stress, because stress is a key issue in this simplifying business.

As we all know, our bodies, like those of all other animals, are beautifully designed to handle stress. As soon as a stressful situation happens, especially a dangerous or frightening one, there is a cascade of changes which takes place in the body, quite automatically. The heart beats more quickly, oxygen uptake increases, certain hormones are released, blood flow changes in certain ways, making us instantly ready to perform the actions appropriate to the situation. These animal bodies of ours are programmed to flee, to fight, to freeze – whichever is likely to work best in the situation (and /or, in the case of females, whose bodies also release oxytocin under stress, to gather up the children and huddle with other females for safety and moral support). So elegant is the body's autonomic nervous system, that performing the necessary action restores everything to equilibrium. The heartbeat slows again, breathing returns to normal, enzymes soak up excess hormones and the animal goes back to grazing quietly, or whatever it was doing before the emergency.

The problem is that many of our modern stressors are mental rather than physical. Say your boss appears at the corner of your cubicle and yells at you that the report should have been on his desk yesterday. Your body, which has a limited selection of software, selects and runs what it thinks is the appropriate programme, which is the one labelled *emergency>sabre-toothed tiger>dealing with*. However, performing the necessary action (e.g. saying "Sorry, sir, I'll have it ready for you by nine in the morning," through clenched teeth) doesn't do a whole lot to get your equilibrium back. Thumping him might, but that is probably not a wise option.

This is another reason why physical exercise is crucial, for vigorous walking, cycling, swimming, etc. go a long way towards bringing our autonomic nervous systems back into balance.

Because of our ever-active minds, we create even more stress for ourselves by our internal judgements. The frogs in that swamp were putting more decibels of noise out into the night air than all the noisy campers, barking dogs, screaming children and generators put together, yet we slept peacefully. What had really stressed us in those other campgrounds was our own judgement that people in campgrounds should show consideration to others and refrain from making a noise at night.

It is hard to steer clear of such judgements, of course. But in cases like that, it's handy to remember the well-known "Serenity Prayer," i.e. to pray for "The serenity to accept the things I cannot change, the courage to change the things I can and the wisdom to know the difference." Faced with a noisy campground, if I can't do a Dalai Lama and summon some genuine serenity, then I have a range of options, from short-term ones like using earplugs or asking the offenders to be quiet, through medium-term ones like shifting to another spot or complaining to management, to long term ones like campaigning for curfews in campgrounds. Simply lying in my sleeping bag, muttering and swearing, creates stress I cannot discharge and so is bad for my health.

What I have hoped to show by these examples is that the closer we can stay to the trunk and main branches of the tree, the easier it is to trace our way to the right twigs and leaves. So the process goes like this:

1. What is good for the cell is good for the planet
2. The health of my own cells is therefore essential
3. So physical health is one of the tree's main branches
4. Since I am an animal, I must care for my animal body
5. To care for my animal body, I must follow its laws
6. To follow its laws I must understand its basic mechanisms
7. One of its basic mechanisms is the stress-coping mechanism
8. The stress-coping mechanism is designed to restore equilibrium
9. Since modern life doesn't always allow automatic return to equilibrium –

10. I must find my own ways to ensure that equilibrium is always regained

That process gets me right to the place where the twigs and leaves of my own, individual decision-making begin. Exactly what those twigs and leaves are will depend on the particular circumstances of my life. But they could be things like, for example:

• Build in to my daily routine at least forty minutes of vigorous exercise every day

• See less of Person X because I find her company stressful, or –

• See more of Person X so that I get to know and understand her better, thereby (perhaps) becoming less judgmental of her behaviour

• Practise relaxation techniques

• Say no to a promotion that will increase my workload

• Replace sugary drinks with water, herbal tea and pure fruit juice

• Listen to my favourite music instead of watching a violent film

• Read a book on assertiveness techniques, which will help me to feel less powerless and therefore reduce my rage level

We have taken our first look at the "how" of simplifying, using the tree analogy to give us a logical method to follow. And we have started looking at where these new ideas might fit into our lives, where the changes and adjustments need to be made, etc.

What about the "when?"

Only you can decide on a time scale, since only you know the circumstances of your life and what is involved in changing it.

If you are the sort of person who thrives on colour-coded flow-charts, time-lines, deadlines, tick sheets and all the other paraphernalia of logical planning, now is the time to start drawing up a master plan of action, complete with goals and objectives, dates and targets. Set it all out, print up a copy, pin it up on the wall and refer to it regularly, ticking off the goals as you achieve them, making sure you are sticking to the plan and perhaps even rewarding yourself with gold stars or fair-traded chocolate.

On the other hand, if you are the sort of person who likes to drift gently into new ideas, to set your eyes on a star and then just float in that newly chosen direction, according to the winds and tides, there's no need to make a chart. Instead, you could draw a mandala, in bright colours, with a few key words in it. Maybe cut out or draw a picture or symbolic representation of yourself living the sort of simple life for which you yearn – a man fishing by a stream, a woman pruning roses, a dolphin swimming free, a tree... And pin that on the fridge instead.

Either way, if you are serious about creating a simpler life than the one you have now, then it is important to take the first step as soon as possible, while you are in the mood. Start right now, by making one small (symbolic perhaps) change to your life in the direction of greater simplicity. Just one leaf. Today. Like a tiny piece of yeast in the big bowl of your life, that is enough to start the process going. From here on, anything could happen. You will have planted the seed of sweet simplicity. Soon, you will feel it begin to sprout.

(But whatever you do, no matter how keen you are to start simplifying, please don't put your house on the market till you have finished the next two chapters.)

Lilypad Principle 3

Sensory Awareness is the Key to Delight
Coming to your senses and learning to stay switched on to life

The highly-evolved, human brain is so clever and complex that it can take in millions of bytes of data per second. Like a computer, it can download information, sort it, interpret it and store it, while performing several other unrelated functions at the same time.

However, like the computer, it can only display a certain amount of its stored information on the screen at any one time.

Think about your left, big toe. Feel the skin on it and what is touching that skin right now. How does your left, big toe feel, right this minute? What are the sensations in it?

I'll bet that in the five minutes before you turned this page you were absolutely not conscious of the state of your left big toe. It was totally out of your awareness until I drew your attention to it, correct?

Because of the millions of bytes of data available to our sense organs at any given moment, we have perfected the art of selecting only the most relevant and tuning out the rest. Even a loud noise can be tuned out if it goes on long enough. Ask anyone who lives by a railway station if they hear the trains. I lived right beside a railway station for over a year and the only train I ever noticed, and even that only occasionally, was the goods train that thundered through at two in the morning. The every-twenty-minutes passenger trains, I stopped hearing after two weeks in that house.

In the noisy campground, amongst the revellers and the generators, it was our grumbly, self-righteous judgements which kept us awake. Next to the swamp, we slept peacefully through the frog concert.

A client once telephoned me late at night, stressed out and tearful, to say she was going nuts because the tap on her shower had broken and the shower would not stop running. She had tried turning it off at the mains but the tap fed four apartments and her neighbours insisted on turning it back on again. What should she do? I suggested that she imagine she was camping in a beautiful forest, right next to a waterfall. I spent five minutes painting a word-picture of the scene, ferns and all. She went back to bed and later told me that she had slept happily through the rest of that night.

What we display on our screens of moment-by-moment awareness will be selected to fit the moment, shaped by our thoughts and judgements, filtered by its degree of familiarity and chosen for its usefulness to us right at that time.

One of the chief problems of modern life is that so much of our bodily awareness gets filtered out. It gets filtered out because it is so familiar (like the sound of the trains) and because it might get in the way of our "important" mental processes, like thinking, obsessing, planning, worrying, strategizing, etc. We train our hunter-gatherer bodies to keep quiet about their needs, to wait out of sight while we write our reports, make our deals, check our e-mail, watch the stock market, balance the books, stand in line, hassle with the traffic. This ability to tune out the needs of our bodies and not to hear the first whispers of trouble can make us sick.

Another aspect to this dulling of our sensory awareness is that we lose one of the most important sources of pleasure which we, as animals, have: sensory appreciation.

My daughter and son-in-law once had a beagle. She was a delightful, good-natured dog and friendly, too. But the most memorable thing about her was her passion for sniffing. She lived for the joy of smell. When I took her for a walk, she ran excitedly from one smell to the next, her whole body quivering with delight.

They brought her to visit us when she was just a puppy. So thrilled was she to have all this new territory to sniff that she almost exploded from sheer excitement.

One can only imagine the magnificence of that little dog's olfactory experience. But we, too, have a sense of smell which deepens and becomes more powerful and discriminating, the more we use it. (Think of a wine-taster.)

We have the miraculous ability to see, and the more we use our eyes, the more delight they give us. Think of a mother, watching her new baby as it suckles, or a diver in wide-eyed exploration of the colour and magic of a coral reef. Think of the majesty of mountains, the pageant of a sunset, the vastness of a starry night or the amazing world in a drop of pond water under a microscope.

Then there is the hunger of our skin for touch, there is erotic delight, there is the exuberance of movement and dance, and the joy brought to our ears through music and song. Think of all we are missing in any moment that we are not fully in our sensing bodies. Add up all the moments, the hours, days, weeks, we spend caught up in our thoughts or spaced out in front of the virtual worlds of our TVs and computers and switched off to the vast treasure house (and pleasure house) of sensory awareness.

When sensory awareness is dulled like that, we find ourselves seeking more dramatic thrills on the TV – more car chases, more shoot-outs on rooftops – in a vain attempt to wake ourselves up. Yet all we really need in order to feel fully alive is to open the doors of perception again and come back into the fullness of our hunter-gatherer senses.

So Step 3 on our list of steps is to practise sensory awareness. There are two important reasons for this step. The first is that by tuning in at ever-deepening levels to the hunter-gather body in which you walk around, you will be better able to hear the early whispers of distress and make the necessary adjustments before a whisper becomes a shout. The second is that when you are operating with all your senses fully switched on, food becomes tastier, flowers are more fragrant, textures more rich, music more sublime, beauty more amazing, and your sex-life improves a hundredfold. In other words, ordinary life can become so miraculous and so filled with delight that you will wonder why you ever bothered with TV.

It would be unfair of me not to mention the downside, which is that the more wide awake all your senses are, the more sensitive you become. Things which never bothered you before – loud music, the chemicals in synthetic perfumes, stuffy rooms, cigarette smoke, tight collars and waistbands, TV commercials, high-heeled or pointy-toed shoes and a million other things – might start to irritate you. But even that is not really a downside. In fact, it is wonderful. What better barometer could you dream of than one like that, which tells you exactly where and how you need to simplify your life? Stay out of discos, stop using "fragranced" products, open all the windows, quit smoking, (and avoid smoky pubs) wear comfortable clothes made from natural fibres, switch off TV, and every stressful annoyance on that list will melt away. And your life will be simpler than ever.

Chapter Four

"The Reservoir"

I have just realized what that memory is – the one which has been trying to resurface. It has to do with duckweed.

That bright, green duckweed on the pond reminds me of a recurring nightmare which plagued me for all of my childhood and well into my adult years.

In a remote corner of the park where my mother took me walking as a child, there was an ancient and long-abandoned reservoir. It was surrounded by trees and a tangle of scrub and brambles, and its surface was totally covered in thick, green duckweed. The old reservoir both fascinated and terrified me. Whenever I saw it, or even thought about it, a shiver of fear would run right through me.

In my nightmare, I fell into the reservoir. But rather than being covered with green plants, the water itself was green and viscous, like pea soup. I struggled to swim, flailing in panic, until I awoke in a sweat, my heart pounding.

Sometimes, the water was a different colour, red or brown or even white. But it was always thick and opaque. For some reason, that quality of opacity was, for me, profoundly terrifying.

In middle adulthood, after I became interested in psychology, psychotherapy and meditation, and began to explore the mysterious depths of my own mind, the nightmares gradually diminished. The further I penetrated into the unconscious, discovering, and learning to befriend, the ancient fears and troubles which had lurked there for years, the less often those dark dreams of struggling in thick water happened. Eventually, to my relief, they stopped altogether.

One night, some time in my fiftieth year, I dreamed of the reservoir again. This time, however, there was no fear. It was the very same reservoir, but now it was empty, and I was crawling around on my hands and knees on the still-damp bottom, amongst little pools and still-wet patches of green slime. Here and there were small, strange, unidentifiable amphibians; unusual, land/sea creatures, at home in the depths but equally at home on land, in the light and air. I crawled around amongst these little creatures, greeting them. This time, instead of waking in panic, I opened my eyes to a feeling of profound peace.

I have never seen the reservoir, or anything like it, in my dreams again since that night.

A few years later, when I was studying with a well-known teacher of shamanism, the class was invited to select an entry point for a journey to the Lower World. With no hesitation I knew where my spot should be. I closed my eyes and, as the drumming began, I found myself once more at the edge of the reservoir in the park. Trembling, I stood on the edge. Why on earth had I chosen this awful place? But I knew it was the right one. Taking a deep breath, I dived straight into the duckweed, swam down through the murky depths, and came out into the Lower World, where my "power animals" were waiting to greet me. It was a profound and powerful experience.

When I returned, a few years ago, in this ordinary reality, to that park of my childhood, the reservoir was long gone. It is just a grassy hollow nowadays, with benches under shady trees. But that place served me well. It taught me the immeasurable value of diving deep.

Discovery – The Growth Spiral

For the first thirty-odd years of my life, I thought "growth" was just a physical thing – something plants and animals do until they reach maturity, at which point they stop growing and start getting old. Sort of like climbing a mountain, sitting on top for a while to enjoy the view, and then starting down the other side. That was, I see now, a very two-dimensional concept.

In my thirties, I started reading pop psychology books and discovered phrases like "personal growth" and "spiritual growth," which were all about getting rid of one's dysfunctional behaviour patterns (psychospeak for what used to be called "bad habits") and becoming a better, smarter, wiser, nicer, more efficient, more prosperous and more successful and loveable person.

I was naïve enough to believe that after all that shifting and tweaking of the psyche and all that growing and improving, and all that money paid out for workshops, meditation tapes and therapy sessions, one eventually reached a sort of finished state – like a house that's been renovated and is now ready to live in.

But of course, it doesn't work like that, as anyone will know who has spent a fortune on self-help books and yet still browses the self-help section of the bookstore, hoping to kick-start yet another personal growth spurt.

Let's face it, it doesn't even work like that in home renovation. Not very often, anyway. Most of us are forever fiddling with our homes: adding bits on, laying new carpet, installing a new furnace, painting, plastering, pointing the brickwork, changing the colour scheme, rearranging the furniture.

There is nothing strange or unnatural about that. Other animals do it too; beavers constantly do dam improvements, badgers add new rooms to their setts, bower birds build bigger and better bowers.

Have you noticed that none of them ever seem to downshift? You never see a bower bird piling a third of his collected items into a black plastic bag and carting it off to a charity shop.

The urge to tinker and improve, to expand territory and to grow, grow, grow, seems to be hard-wired into most species, including ourselves. Which of course is why Homo sapiens has spread over the entire face of the globe and is now taking up so much room and using up so many resources that we have reached a point of ecological crisis. In a way, we couldn't help it. We were just following our inner urges. Beavers would have done the same if they'd had the opportunities and the adaptability that our genes conferred on us.

We have grown in two ways: outwardly and inwardly. Our outward growth is the expansion of human populations. It is a growth in quantity. Our inward growth, on the other hand, is not a quantitative but a qualitative growth. It is a growth of complexity, both of our brains and of our lifestyles.

For our cave-dwelling ancestors, dinner was freshly-caught game or gathered berries, etc., eaten with the hands, sitting on the floor of the cave. For us, dinner has a huge infrastructure that includes working, shopping, paying bills, a kitchen, a stove, several cupboards, a refrigerator, table and chairs, gadgets, crockery, cutlery, linen, salt, pepper, spices, tomato ketchup and on and on...

As our physical lives have become more complex over the centuries, there has been a corresponding increase of complexity in our mental lives.

When humans lived in a tribal setting, in an oral culture where the wisdom and knowledge of the group was held in the form of stories, embedded in the landscape and transmitted from generation to generation, I fancy people's mental lives were far less complex. Maybe back then it really was like I used to imagine – a growth to full maturity and then a slow slide down towards old age and death.

But as the cerebral cortices of our brains developed more and more convolutions and we became more and more adept at self-reflection, introspection and abstraction, we reached the point where we began to realize that the potential for "personal growth" was virtually limitless.

So the individual, nowadays, who embarks on a voyage of inner discovery, can go on sailing the seas of the psyche for a lifetime and never reach the end of the journey.

In fact, the metaphor of the ocean voyage is apt. For like the sailor on our round planet, our journey seems to take us in circles.

This was what I began to notice as I got more deeply into psychology and into my own journey of personal growth. Landmarks I had seen before suddenly appeared on the horizon again. Emotional issues I thought I had resolved started popping up again. Was I simply treading water, kidding myself that I was "improving" myself yet in fact not improving at all?

It was then that I discovered the growth spiral.

All life, as we know, is cyclic: rising and falling; growing and waning; moving in rhythm with the days, the seasons, the circling moon, the spinning of the Earth on its axis. Yet at the same time, as I said before, we are constantly evolving, changing, complexifying. If you combine a circular movement with a forward movement, you get a spiral.

I realized that, on my personal growth journey, when issues I have looked at before come round again, they seem nevertheless to come around in some slightly more refined form. It is a bit like sanding furniture. You start with coarse sandpaper, then a slightly finer grade and then finer still and so on, and you keep sanding the same surfaces of the same chest of drawers. With each turn of the spiral, problems feel as though they are getting resolved at deeper and deeper levels.

All of us, in some way, are moving forward together in our development as a species, deepening in our inner complexity. And we are also living in a circling, cycling world – a world of constant flux and change.

The trick to living with this spiral tide, I believe, is to understand and flow with it. So, as with any other journey we take, the journey to the simple life – for each of us as individuals and for us all as a society – will be a spiral movement, forward and around, stopping and going, sometimes wobbling and wavering, but ever deepening. It's a journey which may never end.

Step 4
Diving Deep

As we discussed earlier, physical pain and discomfort are not bad. They are our friends and guides. They come into our lives as signposts, pointing the way. Tourists are often amused by the fact that in Australia, at the ramps of freeways, they have a sign that points in the opposite direction, aimed at anyone foolish enough to try and traverse the ramp in the wrong direction. It is a big, red sign that says **"Wrong Way. Go Back!"** Pain is that sort of sign.

Likewise, if we start looking more closely at the way we have been living, we shall discover other types of signposts pointing to a deeper disharmony in, or dissatisfaction with, the life we have been telling ourselves we should lead. These are not physical signposts but mental and/or emotional ones.

One of these – and it is a really good type of signpost to read – is the one that points to our so-called "bad habits." Those behaviours which, (before we parked the "blame" vehicle), we used to label as bad, may in fact be holding messages for us that we would do well to decipher. So we can take a look back at those now, without blame this time, but in the spirit of scientific curiosity.

"Bad habits" are no accident. They have developed for a reason, and it pays to investigate what that reason might have been.

We dimly understand this in our children although, even there, we often miss the deeper message. Truancy, for example, or "bad behaviour" in the classroom are likely to be seen as problems with a child or even with a parent, rather than as a symptom of the way the entire education system is failing our children. After all, no toddler ever played truant from playtime. No-one runs away from something interesting, stimulating and fun. No child willingly chooses angry attention over joyful, loving attention. So if school is not interesting, stimulating and fun, it is hardly the children's fault.

With our own "bad behaviour," most of us are merely critical and punitive. We all have an "Inner Critic," a voice that nags, complains and criticizes, constantly harping at us for not performing as well as we think we should.

Many books have been written about how this harsh, inner voice came to be there, and how to deal with it. But for our purposes, right now, it could be handy to tune into it. For the Inner Critic will be delighted to list all our bad habits for us, if we ask it, which will save us having to dig for them.

We need to know what these habits are. (Be careful, though; listen to the list without getting back into "blame" mode. This is an experiment: not a telling-off session.)

> *If you feel like it, take your pen and paper and make a list of all those things about yourself which you have, in the past, thought of as your "bad habits". List especially those you have been trying to "fix" for years, to the point of exasperation.*

In our lists, there may be good clues to the direction that our new journey, the journey of simplification, needs to take. Let's look at an example:

My all-time favourite "bad habit" is procrastination, so that is at the top of my list. I set to work to study it. Why do I put things off? Well it may be a sign that I am trying to make myself do something that deep down I don't want to do.

Of course, there's an equal chance that it may not. So I need to look at this phenomenon a little more closely and see what sorts of things I put off...

I notice, as I look at the things on my list, that some of the activities I put off are actually things I like doing. This seems rather weird. But I am not alone; I have often heard people say that they like writing letters but for some mysterious reason it is hard to get the pen and paper out and actually write. I can be pottering around in the kitchen, the deadline for an article or book review is looming, yet I find myself reorganizing the kitchen cupboards instead of switching on the computer. But once I do start, I'm fine.

What underlies this weird behaviour?

I spend a lot of time puzzling over this until I remember that in High School physics we learned about the law of inertia. Remember that one? Roughly translated, it says that it takes less energy for an object to stay in the state it is in than to switch to another state. A ball that is sitting still needs energy of some kind applied to it in order to start rolling. By the same token, a ball that is rolling needs some form of energy applied to it in order to stop in its tracks.

So some of the things I put on my list might not be procrastination at all but just inertia. I cross those things out.

I also cross out things like dentists and income tax returns, which have to be done but which nobody likes doing. No mysteries there. That leaves me with things I only *think* I have to do. Those are the ones I home in on.

This turns out to be a rich vein to be mined for ways in which to simplify my life. Every item on that *"have* to do" list gets a reality check.

Whenever I discover an item in which the "have to do" is something imposed on me by myself and not an outside force (like an employer or the Government) or something that is done for normal health or safety reasons (like checking smoke alarms or flossing my teeth), then I submit that item to a fierce interrogation. *Is it really true* that I have to do this? What would be the consequences of not doing it? Where did the rule come from? Who made it and why? What are the payoffs for doing it that I am reluctant to lose?... and so on.

Once I am clear that this item could, theoretically, be removed from my life and that I really would like it removed, then all that remains is to work out how and when to take the necessary steps – and how to deal with the consequences.

This is the point, by the way, at which a simplicity circle comes in handy. (We shall talk more about those in Step 6.) Having a brainstorm about this sort of problem can be really useful. Others in the group may have faced a similar issue and can say how they did it, what happened as a result, and how they felt.

If procrastination is one of your "bad habits" also, you might try this for yourself: First make a list of all the things you put off doing.

Cross out any which could be redefined as simply inertia.

Next, cross out examples of things (like the dentist one) which have to be done, regardless.

Analyze the rest carefully. Do you really have to do that thing, whatever it is? Why? What would be the consequences of not doing it?

In this list, some opportunities for simplification will almost certainly be lurking. What if, for example, you have listed "writing out all the Christmas cards"? Unlike a visit to the dentist (which is important for your health) and doing taxes (which is required by law), sending Christmas cards may be a habit you would actually like to cut out of your life, if only you could figure out how to go about it.

I have found another category on my own list. I call this one "mystery procrastination." This is where I procrastinate about doing something which I don't consciously dread doing. It may even be something which I think I shall enjoy, but more often it is something about which I think I'm neutral.

For example, I was President of a committee. The meetings were jolly and pleasant yet I was invariably late for them, even though I'm normally punctual. Tasks I had eagerly agreed to take on somehow got put off and put off. As time went on, I found myself increasingly reluctant to go to the meetings yet without understanding why. Finally, I did some "self-therapy" around it (see Appendix A for the method I used) and discovered that it was actually my need to feel important which kept me there. Underneath, I resented the time I had to spend. So I resigned. I continued to do voluntary tasks for that group sometimes, but only when I felt like it. My life became a lot simpler, and less stressful, as a result.

As Freud discovered, our conscious mind is only the tip of an iceberg. Below the surface is a whole lot of material which is much harder to access. Some of it may be almost inaccessible – such as really traumatic memories which we have blanked out and which can only be reached by, for example, hypnosis. But most of it is not all that difficult, really. It is simply a matter of taking time out to sit with it and make the connections.

It is important to do so because the feelings and impulses which arise from this secret area of the mind are often some of the most powerful ones in our lives; they influence our everyday behaviour quite drastically. There may be things in there which could sabotage our efforts to simplify our lives. We need to get more familiar with these deeper levels of ourselves. There are many ways to do it, thousands of books to tell us how and millions of therapists ready and willing to help us – for a fee. But, as a therapist of many years' experience myself, I assure you that you can quite easily do most of it yourself, for free. (See Appendix A.)

As you can see from the above example, by analyzing more deeply something you have always thought of as a "bad habit", you can sift out important information about yourself and why you feel the way you do about certain things. That information can help you find more ways to simplify your life.

Here, we have looked at just one of these common "bad habits": procrastination. But you can do something similar with any of them.

For example, another of mine is that I can be very critical and judgmental. I tend to find fault with people, in my mind anyway, even if I do not criticize them overtly. When I look closely at this pattern, I discover that my judgment is often a cover for something else– usually envy. Here are some illustrations:

Critical comment: *"He is not pulling his weight."*
Hidden envy: *"I wish I could chill out like he does and not spend all this time fussing over how things are done."*
Possible action: look at why I want this project to be perfect. Is this a case where "good enough" will do? If it is, ease up. If not, acknowledge and fully own my envy and get on and do the best job I can.

Critical comment: *"She is a spendthrift."*
Hidden envy: *"I wish I didn't feel so obliged to think carefully about every tiny purchase I make."*
Possible action: acknowledge the envy. Remind myself that I am doing what feels like the right thing but that not everyone is ready to join me yet, and that is OK.

Critical Comment: *"All they ever report is bad news."*
Hidden Envy: *"I wish I were one of those people who didn't feel the world's pain so keenly."*
Possible Action: be kind to myself. Stop buying newspapers and watching TV shows that sap my energy. Don't feel guilty about not reading and listening to all the horrid stuff. I shall be even more effective if I am not ground down into despair every day by the media, which thrive on bad news.

As you can see, with just three examples taken at random, I have already sifted out at least one item that could greatly simplify my everyday life – ignoring the mainstream media.

Every one of our so-called "bad habits" has been developed for a reason. Often, we developed them at a young age, in order to adapt as best we could to our surroundings. I knew a man who, as a child, learned to run and hide whenever his father came home drunk and angry. It was a good strategy. For if he was around when Dad came lurching through the door, he would usually get beaten with a leather belt, for no reason whatsoever. As an adult, whenever life got difficult, and especially if his wife became angry about something, this man would "run and hide," either to the pub or into a sulky silence. But his adaptive strategy, ideal for surviving at the age of ten, was ruining his marriage at thirty-five.

Once he realized this, he was able to thank the Child within him for finding a way to survive those early years, and then to adopt a new coping strategy more appropriate to who he was now.

You might like to look back, now, at your own list of "bad habits". Assume that each one of them serves (or has once served) a useful purpose in your life.

Taking each in turn, turn it over like a penny and examine the other side of it.

Is it masking some other feeling? Is anger masking fear, irritation masking weariness, snappiness masking sadness, greediness masking fear of scarcity? Is selfishness a form of self-protectiveness and laziness a sign of boredom?... and so on.

What was the original "good" reason for developing this behaviour? Is there a hidden message in it somewhere?

Use your creativity, your imagination – and, above all, your compassion towards yourself – to decipher the deeper meanings. Then look for the signposts that tell you the direction in which you need, and want, to go.

At the deepest level of all in your unconscious mind are what I have called the "need-holes." The reason they are at the deepest level is because they formed there during your first few hours, days, weeks, months or years of life. The earlier they formed, the more deep-seated and pervasive they are and the stronger their influence on your life and behaviour as an adult. And the earlier they formed, the harder they are to articulate when you do unearth them, since they were created before you had any other language than a baby's anguished cry in which to express your unfulfilled needs.

When I think of need-holes, I often think of Ralph.

Ralph was a strong, macho sort of man, a policeman whose work took him into many tough places and situations. It was exhausting, but Ralph was even more exhausted than his colleagues, for he was also moonlighting – doing a second job to bring in more money in order to service a crippling mortgage and several personal loans, taken out to support a lifestyle that his policeman's salary could not stretch to cover.

When I first met him, Ralph's world had finally collapsed. His marriage had ended under the strain of it all, his wife had left, and he was suicidal and in total despair.

He sat in my office and berated himself: for not working hard enough; for not being strong enough; for giving up and, above all, for losing his wife. It was only when I asked him to imagine his wife sitting in the other chair and to talk to her that he stopped chiding himself for his unworthiness and began to cry instead. As the first tears gradually gave way to deep, heaving sobs and eventually to a heart-rending wail, Ralph touched, for the first time in forty years, the memory of standing at the rail of his cot, crying for a mummy who (because she was busy trying to run a shop) never came to comfort him.

All of Ralph's frenetic efforts to surround himself with things – the fancy house, the swanky car, the Armani suits, not to mention a busy, busy life which left no time for reflection and no time to notice that he was in a loveless marriage – revealed themselves for what they really were. All had been attempts to fill an unfillable need-hole: his Inner Child's deep-seated yearning to be held.

Once he had touched into that deep space, Ralph understood what had been driving him. He'd had a direct experience of the need-hole in his psyche. Moreover, he knew, with his logical, adult mind, that a need-hole, like a leaking bucket, can never really be filled, but only understood. After that, he learned to take better care of that little Inner Boy, to acknowledge him when he whimpered, and to cherish rather than berate him. His lifestyle changed; he moved to a smaller house, a different job and eventually found a new and loving partner with whom to share his now simpler and so much sweeter life.

As with Ralph, crisis will often reveal these need-holes. But we can also trace our way back to them by looking at our everyday wants and desires. Why do I want to eat chocolate cake? Why do I want another pair of shoes? Why did I say "yes" to that task when I am already so busy? Is it that I need to be needed? To feel important? To be noticed? Why do I need that?

I once saw a film about binge eating entitled "Looking in the Fridge for Feelings". It's a pattern we all recognize. Feeling upset? Eat chocolate. Need more love? Go shopping. It is hard to move towards a simpler life if you have not yet begun to uncover your need-holes, for your hungry, needy, wailing Inner Child will do his or her best to sabotage your efforts otherwise.

Once you meet that Child directly, you can begin to cherish her or him in direct ways instead. A small child's needs are for things like love, attention, fun, learning... all *simple* things.

This getting-to-know-yourself-better, deep-diving into stuff, is the hardest part of the work. It is never totally complete, for any of us, so you don't have to complete it before moving on to Step 5. It is enough to know about it, and how to do it.

The whole point of doing this deep-diving work right now is to bring, both consciously and unconsciously, your own, personal growth process into full alignment with your goal of creating a simpler life for yourself. Which means that from now on, each time you discover something new about yourself, with that discovery will come another opportunity for simplifying your life.

Lilypad Principle 4
We Can Trust the Process
Flowing with change and uncertainty

This sounds like a stupidly obvious statement: if you take steps to simplify your life, then things, maybe lots of things, are going to change.

For most of us, change is deep-down scary, whether we admit it or not. So one of the important steps we need to take on this journey is consciously to acknowledge change, honour it as a natural process of the Universe and relax around it.

The Zen teacher, Charlotte Joko Beck, once said our human lives are a bit like those mini-whirlpools you often see here and there in a river, when the water is running over stones. Each mini-whirlpool is a separate little entity, yet it is also part of the river. The whirlpools come and go. There are always some there, but they appear in different places on different days.

Those who have studied quantum physics understand that although we perceive the world as being full of solid objects, at the most elementary level there's no such thing as solid matter. Everything that exists (including ourselves) is just a collection of atoms and whirling electrons – a dance of pure energy.

Nevertheless, we cling to the notion of solidity because it feels more...well, *solid*. Solidity makes us feel more secure, and most of us spend our whole lives seeking security: we fix burglar alarms to our houses; pay into pension plans; take out insurance against loss, damage or death; install firewalls on our computers; teach our children not to talk to strangers; vaccinate the whole family (including the cats and dogs) against dire diseases; and are forever saying "take care". We cling to the familiar, to the known, to the safe, and we worry lest some part of the safe, secure wall we have created around ourselves might suddenly break off and plunge us into the chaos of unexpected change. We resist ageing, dread accidents, fear sickness and disability, and try not even to think about death.

Instinctively, though, we know that solidity, safety, security, pre-dictability and sameness are all the stuff of illusion. Our individual lives are, indeed, very much like those little whirlpools Joko Beck speaks of: temporary, evanescent things which may flatten out at any moment and become an indistinguishable part of the river once again. It is the deep knowing of that which seems to create some kind of contraction in one's body, a "clutching" feeling in the solar plexus, an ongoing, low-level tension. And it is this which leads to all our frantic efforts to create the illusion of security.

Many of the things which make contemporary life so stressful for so many people, and which are slowly turning us into a popula-tion of sick canaries, are based on these efforts to create security, especially financial security. But all the time we are working eighty-hour weeks in stressful jobs to try and increase our income and sav-ings, buy more stuff, upgrade our houses and cars and keep up with all the latest trends, we are actually mortgaging the present to pay for a future that may never happen and to create something which is, and always will be, an illusion.

Although you often hear people using the expression "Go with the flow", how many of us really do incorporate that idea into every moment of our lives? Yet learning to go with the flow of the river of life is probably the single most transformative, life-changing and joy-making thing we can ever possibly do.

The one thing that we can say with absolute certainty about life is that everything alive is forever changing. So there is no way we can ever relax into the life of peace and simplicity we long for until we really get the message, right inside our bones, that life is change, that everything changes, in every minute and every second, and that we must flow with it and trust that process.

Without that, we can still create somewhat simpler lives than the ones we have now. But if we learn to accept completely, in our bod-ies and minds and hearts, the fact that there is no solidity, no secu-rity, no way of controlling the flow of that river, and so find a way to release the clutching in the solar plexus, then our whole being feels lighter and the path to simplicity suddenly appears as short, straight and lined with primroses.

So Principle No. 4 on the seven-step path to simplicity requires that we incorporate into our lives some kind of spiritual practice which will remind us, every single day, about the impermanence of life, the inevitability and rightness of constant change, and the illusory nature of this seemingly solid world, and will encourage us, every single day, to flow with what is, rather than making futile attempts to hold back the river.

Chapter Five

"The World of Tiny Things"

The wild strawberries have finished now, and almost all the flowers have disappeared. Fallen oak leaves float like tiny brown boats on the bare patch of pond where the autumn wind has blown aside the duckweed.

The pink petals of the campions, which brightened this wild end of my tiny garden throughout all of spring and summer are gone now and in their place are little seed capsules. I fish my hand lens from my pocket, the better to examine them.

This lens is my spyhole into the universe of tiny things, my passport to the world seen by the eyes of hoverflies and bumblebees.

A friend introduced me to this idea, several years ago. From her, I learned that peering through a lens at something seemingly small and insignificant can break our habitual patterns of perception and open up a new and utterly fascinating world. It gave me yet another simple pleasure to add to a life already rich with sensuous delight.

We were walking together, she and I, along a clifftop path, bordered by some very ordinary-looking coastal vegetation, when she suddenly stopped, fished a tiny, folding lens out of a pocket, and knelt down in front of the plants.

I was curious. "What are you looking at?"

"Here," she said. "Have a look through this."

At her direction, I held it close to one of the little, nondescript flowers, as she had done, and brought the flower into focus. What I saw made me gasp. It was not a little, nondescript flower after all; it had become a huge, lush blossom, full and rich, like a Georgia O'Keefe painting. From its depths, bright yellow stamens rose, their tips soft with pollen grains. A minute dewdrop glistened on one of the petals. The petals themselves shone like velvet and all around their edges was a fringe of delicate hairs. A tiny insect stood balanced in one corner of the flower, its antennae quivering.

"Wow!" was all I could say.

"I love small things, you see," my friend said.

After that, I wanted to borrow her lens to peer at everything. A feather, a leaf, a piece of moss. Even the pattern of lines on my hand and the fine hairs on the skin of my arm took on a totally new perspective. Suddenly, a whole new universe had made itself available to me.

How accustomed we are, I thought, to the scale at which we habitually see the world. Yet were we a different size, the world around us would look altogether different. I remembered the movie, *Microcosmos*, which magnified the world of small creatures so that the audience could see it on the same scale as those creatures themselves, and how that had fascinated me. But without going to the cinema, my friend could access that scale of vision any time she wanted to, just with the aid of her lens, and change her entire view of the world. Maybe we should all have one like that, I decided. If we could see things through the eyes of some creature very different from ourselves, and if we could see the incredible beauty that lies just out of range of our ordinary, everyday vision, maybe it would remind us to have more reverence, show more respect, take more care...

So I bought my lens. It magnifies things ten times. It cost me £30 but it is worth every penny, and now I carry it everywhere. What's more, I'm taking great delight in showing it to other people. Maybe eventually I'll strike someone who has no wish to squint into the mysterious depths of dandelions, but that hasn't happened yet. So far, everyone who has peered through it has said "Wow!" and asked to use it again, just as I did. The makers of folding lenses must be wondering where all this new business is coming from, for many of my "converts" have gone straight out and bought themselves one as well. They, too, have become entranced by that amazing world which we all, being the size we are, think of as the world of tiny things.

It is yet another source of delight – and utterly simple.

Discovery – Trade-Offs

One of the most frustrating things I discovered about simplicity is that every time you make a decision to simplify some aspect of your life, up pops a dilemma.

Like some grinning genie that appears, arms outstretched, in the middle of the road, with a pop and a flash of light, here it is, barring your path. You thought you were on your way, but you were wrong. You will take not one step further till this one has been dealt with. It's called the trade-off. And it will drive you crazy, until you have befriended it, that is. And we shall talk about that, later on. Meanwhile, let's look at some of the typical trade-offs you will meet along this path.

The first, and probably the biggest, is the one I foreshadowed when speaking of the paradox. It is the trade-off between convenience and time/energy. Most of the conveniences we have come to take for granted in our twenty-first century world cost time and energy, but it is usually someone else's time and energy. So when my partner and I moved to our thirty acres in the mountains and started creating a home there, we had very few conveniences at all except for a car and small caravan. We built a shed with a tank next to it and caught rainwater from the shed roof. Our first toilet was a hole in the ground. Later, we built a composting toilet. Our time and energy was mostly spent, during those early months, on providing for ourselves the basic necessities which we had taken for granted in the city: a roof over our heads (first a wooden cabin, then a mud-brick house); water to drink; sanitation; light (first candles, then a paraffin lamp, then later, solar panels); heating and cooking facilities (first a fire, then a woodstove and a solar oven). So we had almost zero convenience at first and were using almost all our time and energy taking care of our own, basic needs – the ones at the lowest level of Maslow's pyramid. As time went on, we created more convenience. With the solar power, once again we had light at the flick of a switch, and so on. Eventually, we reached the point where we felt perfectly balanced. We were still living close to the Earth: getting pleasure from growing and preparing our food; baking bread in our stove; composting almost all our waste and putting it back to nourish the soil; drawing energy from the sun; and living far from the noise and pressure of city life. But we had created enough convenience that we now had time and energy left over for other things. We had reached our point of equilibrium, and it felt just right.

Not everyone will achieve equilibrium in as radical a way as we did, by scrapping everything and starting again from scratch. Most would not be able to – and neither would we, had we done it earlier in our lives, with dependent children and no savings. So for most people, simplifying is more a matter of working backwards towards equilibrium, by keeping most of the conveniences one already has, dispensing with a few, and thinking carefully before investing in any more. If you already have a lawn-mower that works (even though you have to pull the cord six times to get it started) why would you need to swap it for a posher version? Maybe it would be better to save the money and simply spend the time and energy pulling that cord. When it finally conks out, you could downsize to an old-fashioned hand mower and get more exercise. (A wonderful type of simplifying is to join the "Earth Gym," finding creative ways to incorporate aerobics, weight-training and stretches into your everyday life.)

Then again, if your children are grown up and no-one needs the lawn to play ball or do handstands on any more, why not invest a little time and energy into converting the lawn to a mini-woodland of shrubs and small trees with a floor of pine bark mulch and some nice boulders? Then you would have created some more habitat for the birds and other creatures, and never have to mow again. What could be more convenient than that?

Some of the trade-offs I discovered in my various versions of the simple life have been in the "lesser of two evils" category. Those are often hard to figure out. For instance, the chemicals in re-charge-able batteries are deadlier than the ones in the disposables, but the former last heaps longer. So is it better to have more of the less deadly chemicals or less of the more deadly ones?

Coal is the most efficient fuel for our old Rayburn stove in the kitchen, but it has to be trucked two hundred miles from the coal mine and it makes a mess, is heavy to cart around in the coal bucket and the soot in the air is bad for my asthma. Oil would be the cheapest fuel, and has no polluting smoke, but that comes from many more hundreds of miles away and the stove would need converting or replacing. Wood is the most local, but the more wood is collected, the less habitat for the other creatures who depend on old logs and fallen trees and the fewer nutrients are left to return to the soil. Besides which, it burns more quickly than coal so we need more of it. Best of all, so far, seems to be the idea of pellets made from sawdust, which are a by-product of sawmills, especially if a local supply-chain can be established, which I'm told is likely to happen soon. However, that option, too, like oil, will probably involve replacing the stove. So now we have to factor in all the energy which goes into creating the new stove and the materials it's made of, and balance that against the energy we are saving by not using coal or oil. Over time, converting to pellets may work out to be the best option. But when the time comes that all the electricity on the grid comes from wind, tide, sunshine or biofuel, then the equation will change again and we shall find ourselves weighing the energy cost of new heating appliances against the benefits of clean, smokeless air.

Like this, many of the trade-offs which pop up along the road to simplicity are difficult ones, constantly shifting and changing as new information and new factors come in. And one may not always make the best or perfect choice. Sometimes, there *is* no perfect choice. But the important thing is this: by stopping each time the trade-off genie appears on the road, and opening a dialogue with it about the pros and cons of where you are going and why, you will be doing something many people are not yet able to do – taking responsibility for the dilemmas of the Earth. Not that you are solving them. How could you do that, single-handed?

But we are all shouldering our share of the burden, simply by thinking about the issues, considering the pros and cons of each decision, and taking what feels to us, after due consideration, to be the best and most eco-friendly way forward that we can manage at this point. That is perhaps the most significant and important step we shall make on this journey – picking up the burden of our share and doing the best we can to carry it. Since many hands, as we know, make light work, if every man and woman on Earth would just do that, all our planet's seemingly intractable environmental problems would soon melt in the warmth of humanity's universal care and concern.

Step 5
Doing it for Ourselves

Some writers say that in creating a simpler life one should look forward, not back. In other words, focus on the life you would like to live from now on, rather than what is wrong with the one you have now.

That would be excellent advice, if we were truly the rational creatures that we like to kid ourselves we are. Trouble is, we are not ruled only by rationality. As I mentioned earlier, our minds are like icebergs, with the rational bit sticking out of the water and all the rest – the infantile needs and desires, the instinctual urges, the unmet needs, longings and unconscious programming and so on – underneath, out of sight. But it is that huge, hidden section under the water that determines much of what we feel, what we say and what we do. It is because that part has an enormous influence on the decisions we make and the directions we take that I am putting so much emphasis, in this book, on the inner journey to simplicity, rather than the outer one. My belief is (and this has been borne out by experience over many, many years) that if you pay attention to those inner things, the outer things will more easily fall into place.

Obviously, then, the more we know about that underwater section of ourselves, the more skilfully we can plot our course. Likewise, the less we know about it, the greater the likelihood that we shall find some aspect of it messing up, or even totally sabotaging, the well-laid plans of our rational minds. Those needy Inner Kids we have spent decades ignoring are the world's best saboteurs!

So yes, we should look forward. We need a vision, for it is a star to steer by. (That's why I asked you to write notes about your ideal simple life.) But we should also look back – at ourselves, our histories, the habits we have developed and why we developed them.

In fact, what we need to do is look both ways at the same time, just as, when we drive, we look in the rear-view mirror as well as ahead.

Here's another "test" that helps us to look both ways. I call it the Woods Test, as it is one devised by Clay & Judy Woods, whose website is a very useful resource for would-be simplifiers (see www.lilypadlist.com for the link):

"... **time is better than money,**" say Clay and Judy. "**Time to enjoy music, read a book, tend a rose garden, pursue a hobby, or visit with friends is far more valuable to us than the money we could accumulate by working long hours instead of enjoying them. This revelation encouraged us to spend less time acquiring things and more time acquiring experiences, insights, and relationships. At the beginning of our own journey down a simpler path, we made a direct link between time and costs. When we asked ourselves, 'Is it worth x hours of work to buy this?', it often wasn't! If we'd rather spend those x hours doing something else, instead of earning funds for the purchase, we didn't buy it. Because, of course, time is better than money.**"

So here's their simple test:

The Woods Test

1. Make a list of the ten activities you enjoy most.
2. Then make another list of the ten activities that occupy most of your time.
3. Compare the two lists.

How much difference is there between your two lists? If there is only a small difference, then that's wonderful. If the difference is large, what is the message?

If you found a large difference between your two lists, the advice to you from this wise couple (who have been practising what they preach for many years now, is: "**Stop going around in circles and head straight toward what you really want to do. It's the wanting that counts. Doing what you want can make having things you want seem a lot less important. When having fewer things leads** to having more time to do what you choose, you just may find you want fewer things!"

Let's stop for a moment, see where we are on this journey.

> *The Sick Canary Test and the Woods Test, along with the other questions you have answered, (and the deep-diving) are by now, I hope, giving you more clues about what you want to change, and what sort of a simple life to aim for.*
>
> *If you haven't already done so, you might like to look back, now, at your notes from Step 1 ("Catching the Bug"). Go over what you wrote then and see if there is anything you would like to add to it, in the light of these various "tests" and the things we have talked about since you wrote it.*
>
> *You would do well to linger over this task a little, especially to sort out which are "twigs and leaves" items and which are speaking to the more general and foundational "trunk and branches" area of yourself and your life.*
>
> *When you notice "trunk and branches" items, think about the possible twigs and leaves of decision and change to which they might lead you.*

Now we need to get clear about precisely what *sort* of a simple life suits you best. One tends to refer to "the simple life" as though there were just one version of it. Yet, as we know, there are as many versions as there are people and "simplifiers" fall into many types.

To help you get clear at the trunk-and-branches level, before you get into the leaves of detail, let's look now at the two main categories of simplicity, which I think of as physical and mental.

Physical simplicity.

Like I did, you may yearn for plain, simple surroundings wherein your basic needs are supplied in very simple ways. With the physically simple life, you will aim to reduce the amount of possessions you own, reduce the floor space you occupy and do without many of the so-called "useful" gadgets. You may still have gadgets, but only ones you absolutely cannot do without. Let's face it, who really needs an electric can-opener or electric carving knife? (Well, someone with carpal tunnel syndrome might, so let's not pour scorn on anything.) Who needs a built-in waste disposal unit in their kitchen sink, an electric blanket, a paper shredder? Someone might, but possibly you don't. A busy restaurant might need an automatic dishwasher, (though it might do someone out of a job) but what family really does? After all, the larger the family, the more hands there are to share the washing-up. Anyway, washing-up can be a meditation, and if several people do it together, a nice time for chatting.

The more gadgets you have, especially electrical or electronic ones, the more things to go wrong, the more spare parts you have to buy and the more hair-tearing you'll do.

But if there's a gadget which makes your work simpler yet without detracting from the enjoyment of your life, then why ditch it? I have no car, no TV, and no washing-machine, but I have a state-of-the-art computer, because as a writer I would be mad not to. Writing with a pencil or a manual typewriter out of some romantic, Luddite notion of the simple life would not be real simplicity, but sheer daftness. My daughter, with twins in cloth nappies, would be equally daft to ditch her washing machine.

Sometimes the trade-offs take a lot of thinking about; bread-makers free up time, have warm, fresh bread ready in time for breakfast and scent out the house beautifully. Yet they deprive us of the slow, sensuous pleasure of kneading dough and the delight of finding it risen, later, in its warm bowl. (My grandmother used to put the bowl to bed with a hot water bottle!)

The more you buy things in bulk, the less packaging you have to deal with (though here's another trade-off, because the more bulk food you store the more storage space and airtight containers you need and the more you have to worry about guarding stuff from mice and weevils).

As with gadgets, so with ornaments. The more silver you have, the more polishing you have to do, the more stuff on top of the sideboard, the more dusting will be necessary, and so on. But if there is something you love to look at or touch, whether it is the cup you won, a grandchild's photo or a favourite teddy bear, then keep it, and enjoy it forever. There are no rights or wrongs here.

Remember, there are always trade-offs. And remember the simplicity paradox – how choosing a simpler life usually entails more activity on your part. Stairs are simpler than lifts, but if you choose stairs you have to walk up them instead of just pressing a button and letting the lift hoist you up.

Given the sort of person you are, and the sorts of things you enjoy, do you think simplifying your life physically would yield you greater pleasure? Let's ask some nitty-gritty questions that will reveal whether what I call "radical, physical simplicity" will work for you:

Questions: Set A

1. Would you delight in the extra exercise and sensual experience involved in , for example, chopping wood, riding a bicycle, kneading dough, sweeping, using a pole lathe, hand-sanding old furniture?
2. Does reading about people doing those sorts of things or seeing pictures of them give you a feeling of excitement, pleasure or envy?
3. Do you feel a yearning for more exertion and the kind of weariness that comes at the end of a day of physical labour?
4. At those times in your life when you have done that sort of work, or when you have shaped something by hand instead of buying it, did that feel especially satisfying to you?
5. Do you go camping and enjoy the simplicity of a tent and a campfire (or even a caravan) and then find yourself slightly averse to all the demands of a modern house when you return?
6. Do you love taking trips to places far away from telephones and television, where mobile phones don't work?
7. Were you a boy scout or a girl guide and do you remember, with pleasurable nostalgia, what fun it was to go tracking, to make campfires, cook damper, collect firewood, make "gadgets" by lashing sticks together?
8. Do you enjoy gardening? Cooking? Sewing? Crafts?

If you said "yes" to all or most of those questions, you are a likely candidate for radical, physical simplicity. If you said "no" to most of them, you will need to think carefully before implementing anything which simplifies your life physically. You must watch that you don't simplify in ways which will create chores you later come to resent. Or chores which, one day, you may be physically unable to do. (If osteo-arthritis sets in, will you still be able to chop wood and ride your bike?)

Mental Simplicity

It is wonderful to have this highly-convoluted cerebral cortex which gives us the ability to think abstractly, conceptualize, be self-reflective and do all those special things with our minds.

But it has a downside; we can think ourselves into a lather of worry, imagining catastrophes that may never happen. We spend a huge proportion of our lives thrashing around in our memories, doing endless post-mortems on events long gone. "Oh if I had only said XX, then YY might never have happened." When we are not doing that, we are projecting ourselves into the future. "If I do XX, than maybe YY will happen. On the other hand, if I do ZZ... yadda yadda... "

I shared my life for nineteen years with a cat called L . He was a large, glossy, black cat with a sweetly affectionate nature and a delightful personality.

We spent most evenings together, curled up cosily on the couch. When bedtime came, I used to scoop him up in my arms and carry him towards the back door. He would snuggle into my chest, purring happily the whole way to the door, and stay that way even when I opened the door and the chill, night air crept around us both. He always kept purring right up to that very last moment when his paws touched the cold, brick paving of the patio. Whereupon he would yawn, stretch, give a tiny little shudder, and stride off purposefully into the night.

A crazy fantasy occasionally came into my head as I watched him make his almost instant adaptation to his changed circumstances. What if our positions were reversed? What if he were a giant cat and I were a tiny human and he had decided that I could spend my evening by his hearth but that I should spend my nights in the shed instead of the house? Can't you just imagine it? By nine p.m. I would be glancing sideways at the clock, wondering how much longer I had left to enjoy the warmth and comfort of the sofa. I would have an ear cocked for the sound of wind or rain, and an intense interest in the weather forecast on TV. I would be watching my master carefully, willing him not to glance at his watch. When the dreaded moment arrived and he stood up and looked at me, my heart would sink. My body would already be contracted against the inevitable and my mind frantically occupied with plans for escape, tales of resentment, or fantasies of revenge.

And yet... when I found myself outside, standing shivering and alone on the patio, with the door shut behind me, and there was no alternative but to accept the situation and simply get on with it, what would I do then? I would get on with it, of course. Just like L. One generally does. So what is the difference, then, between L's experience and my own? It is a difference of at least two hours and a great deal of pleasure. He has enjoyed that time: I would have wasted it.

Over the years, I have tried to live in a personal world which is more like L's – a world of mental simplicity. I have done this by making every effort to stay aware of the present moment and to spend as little time as possible re-hashing the past and/or rehearsing the future. I am getting better at it, but there is still a long way to go.

So what about you?

Questions: Set B

1. Are you a "worrier"?
2. Is your mind constantly troubled by all the things on your mental "To Do" list?
3. Do you ever chastise yourself for "wasting time," or talk about time as if there is not enough of it to go round, as in: "Sorry, I don't have time", "I wish there were more time", "Time got away from me", etc. and so on?

4. Do you take your little child or your dog for a walk and then find yourself tugging on the child's hand or the dog's lead and saying "Come on!" (I have made a study of the people who walk their dogs up and down the lane outside our cottage and how many times they say "Come on!" to the dogs. Usually, it is every time the dog stops to sniff something. Yet the walk is supposed to be for the benefit of the dog. As the Americans say, go figure!)

5. Do you use the word "busy" a lot, e.g. do you find yourself telling others about how busy you are, or using the excuse, "I was/am too busy"?

6. Do you sometimes feel overwhelmed by your own life?

7. Do you spend most of your time either re-hashing the past or rehearsing for the future and find it difficult to keep your mind fully on the "now"?

8. Do you find it almost impossible to sit still and do nothing?

9. Does your mind sometimes feel so overloaded with thoughts that it is hard to focus on just one thing?

10. Do you lie awake thinking at night?

If you find yourself saying "yes" to all or most of these questions, it is likely that you need to do some mental simplifying. (Most of us do.) However, we can do that without necessarily making any changes in our physical surroundings.

So here's a subset of questions:

Questions: Set C

1. Do you ever feel burdened by your possessions and wish you could ditch half of them?

2. Do you feel a huge sense of relief any time you take a pile of stuff to the tip or to the charity shop?

3. Do you detest having surfaces in your house that are cluttered with ornaments, knick-knacks or piles of paper?

4. Do you gaze longingly at pictures of Japanese house interiors with their clean lines and empty surfaces?

5. Do you admire plain, simple furniture / architecture / clothing and dislike ornateness, rococo designs, frills and bows?

6. Does having an untidy desk make it harder for you to work?
7. Do you ever feel as though broken appliances, unpaid bills and unfinished projects have voices and are clamouring as you walk by them?

The reason I am asking these extra questions is that there is a place where physical and mental simplicity meet and overlap. There is a strong connection between physical clutter and mental clutter. Some people live quite happily in cluttered houses. They may not be untidy people, but their houses are crammed with stuff. Every horizontal surface is filled with photographs, ornaments and whatnot, and the walls are thickly hung with pictures. And yet they remain clear-headed and contented. (I often think they must spend ages dusting, but perhaps they enjoy it.) However, for those of us who feel claustrophobic and overwhelmed in such surroundings (or amidst a lot of untidiness) there is a sense in which physical clutter creates mental clutter. And again, mental clutter can often lead us to be untidy, even if only for certain periods which are interspersed with frantic bursts of clearing up.

If you are in this category, you will easily recognize yourself.

OK, here's where the test results help you to select the *overall type* of simple life best suited for you. Ready?

If you have said "yes" to all three sets of questions then, for you, the way forward from here is quite clear. You just need to get rid of a lot of the stuff you currently own and move steadily towards a physically simple life, perhaps by moving to a smaller living space, and a lower-tech existence.

If you have said "no" to the questions in Set A but "yes" to Sets B and C, you may need to think more carefully before you make a move. You may later regret getting rid of your high-tech gadgets because doing so will necessitate work that may soon begin to irk you. You may be ill-advised to swap a centrally-heated home for a cottage with a wood-stove or a place where the kitchen is too small for a dishwasher. You need to de-clutter because your mental busyness and your overfilled surroundings are probably reinforcing each other in a continuing feedback loop.

Simplification, for you, may mean divesting yourself of many of the ornamental things you have surrounded yourself with, but keeping the really useful ones. Aesthetics, for you, need to be a high priority. A decision to redecorate may supply the impetus you need to create a more congenial living space.

For you, the key to living more lightly on the Earth is to stay where you are, keep the things you really love and regularly use and ditch the rest. Then work at minimizing your impact on the environment by:

1. Making a commitment to the "Three Rs": re-using, repairing and recycling.
2. Optimizing energy efficiency in your house – e.g. by better insulation – and perhaps considering a switch to renewable energy sources.
3. Supporting your local economy by shopping locally, joining a LETS scheme, eating what is in season, etc.
4. Downsizing your gift-exchange habits.
5. Thinking hard before making new purchases.
6. Supporting local artists and craftspeople by buying their goods instead of mass-produced ones. This keeps money in your local economy also.
7. Taking careful stock of your travel habits. Maybe switching to a smaller car, taking public transport whenever you can.

(Take the Ecological Footprint Test at the end of this book for more ideas.)

If you have answered "yes" only to the questions in Set B, then your path to simplicity lies not in the physical world around you but in getting a better handle on your runaway mind. For you, the way forward will have much more to do with changing your thinking patterns, your self-image, the stories you tell yourself, the beliefs you hold, etc. than with building a strawbale house or keeping free-range chickens.

As well as the seven points suggested above, you would do well to focus on meditation or other, spiritual practice that calms turbulent thoughts.

De-cluttering will probably make little difference in your case – though it is always worth trying, just to make sure. We often don't know how much our cluttered surroundings are affecting our thoughts and feelings and moods until we try clearing them.

As your self-awareness deepens, you may perhaps discover, as I did, that you are slightly addicted to that very busyness you think you want to reduce.

If you observe yourself very carefully (and absolutely without blame, remember), there is a clue you could look for here. Whenever you hear yourself talk (or write) to anyone else about your busy schedule, your workload, the pressure of time, etc., check for a tiny little feeling that may be lurking around the edges of your consciousness, a little smirk of pleasure, satisfaction – we could even call it smugness or self-righteousness. It's just a flicker, so it's easy to miss. But keep checking, and you may spot it lurking there. If you find it, smile to yourself. You are one of millions.

In that busy workplace I described earlier, part of the group culture involved walking around with armfuls of files, looking harried, and occasionally flopping down near the coffee machine with a huge, melodramatic sigh. I called it the "I'm More Dedicated Than You" Game. One day, someone came to work there who never carried files around, always looked relaxed and never sighed. She went home promptly every afternoon at five-thirty, while everyone else was scurrying about doing unpaid overtime. Guess what? Everyone disliked her and the word soon went round that she wasn't pulling her weight. She got her work done all right. But she didn't fit in because she was like a teetotaller at a booze-up. She was the only member of staff not addicted to stress.

Remember that stress addiction can live quite happily side by side with the longing for a simpler, quieter life, the yearning to spend more time with the family or the longing to veg out in front of TV. We humans are complex creatures, full of paradox and contradiction. So don't be fooled by your surface emotions or by the stories you like to tell yourself and others. Dive deeper.

OK, it is time now to take another look at your "game plan", this time in the light of what you have learned from your answers to these latest sets of questions.

How does the reality of your answers match up with your dream of your ideal simple life? You might like to spend a few moments now, putting all these pieces together and looking at what is likely to work best for you.

Since people vary so much in their personalities, their preferences, their ways of being in the world, we have focused, in this section, on ways that our paths to simplicity might diverge. There is probably more individual difference between human beings than between members of any other species, at least in the mental sphere, simply because we have evolved such complex brains. So it is important to honour these wonderful and fascinating differences and to make a commitment to express our own authenticity and uniqueness in the way that we live our lives, no matter what the Joneses next door are up to.

Before we leave this chapter, though, let's look at something which is equally applicable to everyone – the need to honour the core of sameness which unites us: our basic, animal selves.

Many of the things which make us so sick, so often perplexed and so stressed are those which force us to live in disharmony with that animal nature.

As I said in Step 1, our modern culture is so new, in evolutionary terms, that the bodies we walk around in have not even begun to adapt to it yet. They are animal bodies. They are the bodies of hunter-gatherers, whose eyes and ears and other senses are tuned to the rhythms of the moon and stars, seasons and weather, not to the artificial demands of the modern workspace. We have eyes programmed to respond to the shapes and colours of forest and savannah, trees, earth and open sky. Our bodies and sense organs have co-evolved with the plant world and the wild creatures with whom we share the planet. And our hearts have been tuned by the millions of years that we spent celebrating the cyclical changes of the Earth, the miracle of new life and the return of the migrating birds rather than the Emmys, the Grammys and the Oscars, or even the Olympic Games.

We are adaptable creatures, to be sure. But our ability to adapt is not infinite. Our eyes may have learned to interpret the cityscape really well and can pick out a tandoori take-away in a busy street from the window of a fast-moving car or spot a Number 31 bus from several hundred yards away. But the reason we flock to the park in our lunch hour is because those animal eyes still hunger for the sight of green and the soles of our feet yearn for contact with soft earth. If our lives become too busy to fit in the necessary exercise, or if we spend too high a proportion of our lives inside one of those artificially-lit, "climate-controlled" buildings with their synthetic carpets and Muzak, we shall suffer.

Demanding too much adaptation from these animal bodies is a recipe for sickness. The herons of our dysfunctional, Western culture will snatch our soft, froggy bodies from the pond if we don't honour the needs of this as-yet-unadapted flesh. So it seems clear to me that irrespective of our individual differences, there is a central, all-important rule-of-thumb which can guide all of us on the journey to simplicity, and it is this:

When in doubt, ask the hunter-gatherer within.

Which leads us to our next – and all-important – Lilypad Principle.

Lilypad Principle 5
We Are All Cells of the Living Earth
Thinking like a molecule

I referred to this model of simplicity as The Way of Consciousness. As you will have noticed, this book is very different from all those books on simple living which explain the surface manifestations of the simple life: how to recycle things; live on less money; tie-dye your old T-shirts; clean your windows with vinegar; and stuff like that. Not that those things are unimportant. They are great; I use vinegar a lot too, recycle as much as possible and live comfortably on a minuscule income. But The Way of Consciousness is about simplifying at *all* levels. At the most profound level of all, it is about coming into alignment with that greater whole of which we are a part, i.e. the Earth.

We now know that the primary pattern in the Universe is that of systems within systems within systems.

Whenever I start feeling either self-important or hopelessly insignificant, my favourite way of putting everything back into perspective is to ponder on the thought that we are all "holons". In other words, each of us is a whole which is composed of parts which are also wholes composed of other parts, and so on down, all the way to the subatomic level. Likewise, as well as being wholes, we are also parts: of our families; our networks; our societies; the planet Herself. And of course our beautiful planet, as well as being a whole, is also a part of the solar system which is part of the Milky Way galaxy, and so on, all the way out to the edges of the Universe. There is a wonderful site on the Web called "Powers of Ten" which illustrates this beautifully. (See www.lilypadlist.com for the link.)

You start with a starscape – an artist's impression of the view towards Earth from billions of miles away. With each mouse-click, the distance alters, each time by the power of ten, until you can see our Galaxy, The Milky Way, as photographed by the Hubble telescope. Next, you come to the solar system, with all the planets circling our sun, and then comes an actual photograph of the Earth from space. One more click, and you are seeing an aerial photo of the south-eastern section of the USA. The next click has you hovering over a cluster of buildings and trees, somewhere in Florida. The click after that, and you are looking at the surface of one leaf. And then, as you click again, you are peering through a microscope at the intricate pattern of cells which make up that leaf. From then on, each click takes you deeper and deeper into the structure of the leaf – atoms, subatomic particles... until eventually you are looking at an artist's impression of things too small to see, even with the strongest, electron microscope.

To me, there is no better illustration than this of our role in the scheme of things. We may think of ourselves as unique, separate individuals, and indeed we are. But we are also no more separate than are the molecules separate from that leaf, nor the leaf separate from its tree, the tree from its ecosystem, the ecosystem from the planet. So if each of us is an actual piece of this planet – which we undoubtedly are – then whatever we do to the planet, to other people, other creatures, we ultimately do to ourselves.

If we stayed in constant awareness of this, how could we do anything that contributed to the trashing of the planet? It would be nonsensical, unthinkable, suicidal.

The simple life is the sustainable life. It is the life which best fits in with the ecosystem within which we live. "Survival of the fittest" doesn't mean fighting, struggling or winning wars. "Fittest", in this context, means "most well-suited" or "best adapted to its surroundings", like the frogs in the pond, camouflaged, in their green and brown skins, from the eyes of herons. That is how to survive.

So the best adapted human beings are the ones whose lives are simple, who use all their senses (including the sixth, which I'll talk about in Chapter Seven), who listen best to the needs of their hunter-gatherer bodies, and who know themselves to be cells in the body of the living Earth.

Chapter Six

"The Water Parsnips"

The pond looks more bare today because I have interfered a little. The problem was that the water parsnips were starting to take over. I knew if I left them unchecked, they would create a mat so thick and dense that everything else would be crowded out. So I removed some of them yesterday afternoon.

I notice that the equisetum (horsetail) that I planted on the water's edge has disappeared. But then, who am I to tell it what it should do? Maybe it simply didn't want to live there.

This is an ongoing dilemma for me, in this garden; how much to interfere and how much to let things be as they are.

The garden is on two levels. Down through the middle of it runs an ancient, Devon bank, a wall of stones and earth, covered thickly in ferns and ivy on the shady side and grass and wildflowers on the sunnier side and the top. Brambles and briars tangle themselves in and around everything, and nettles abound. Blackthorn bushes persevere in their efforts to rise again from their cut stumps.

We trim it right down in the early spring and then again at regular intervals. But if we forget, or if we are away for a while, the flowers come out. And then it is too late. Once the bank is alive with campions and buttercups and purple loosestrife, foxgloves are standing tall and the whole thing is covered in a happy throng of bees and butterflies, I can no longer bear to cut it.

The same goes for the self-seeded poppies and bright blue borage that pop up in between the vegetables and the 'volunteer' vegetables themselves, of which there are always many. They seem to grow particularly well in places of their own choosing.

Australian gardening 'guru,' Jackie French, says that we should content ourselves with being able to harvest ten percent of the vegetables and fruit we plant and be happy that all the other creatures who share our space take the remaining ninety percent. After all, they live here too and have done so much longer than us. I like her sentiment. And when I lived in her wide, spacious land and had thirty acres to grow food in, it was easy to follow the 'ten percent rule.' But here, on this crowded island of England, in this tiny cottage with its pocket handkerchief garden, half-shaded by next-door's sycamore, how do I reconcile my desire to share and my love of all things wild with my own need for food?

Yes, it's a dilemma. Nevertheless, through a process of negotiation, of compromise, of dialogue, each growing season we somehow create a solution that works for everybody. Some berries are netted, others are left open to the birds. Some plants are pulled out to bring more light for others to grow better. Some of the comfrey is slashed to make fertilizer and some is left to flower for the delight of the bumblebees (a declining species now, I read recently). And we share space in a friend's large garden, in return for helping her maintain it.

So this morning, I cut out a large patch of the water parsnips and put it, together with some scooped-out duckweed, on to the compost heap to join the piles of weeds and debris from this year's harvest, now already rotting down. I remind myself that the same molecules which formed that thick, green mat on the pond may next year manifest as the blue star of a borage flower, the egg of a wren or the lettuce leaf upon my plate. Bacterium, snail, 'weed', fruit, eagle, woman – we are all of us nothing but an endless, ever-changing, recycling dance of molecules. And molecules are nothing but a dance of energy.

The tiny, open patch of water is sparkling in the late autumn sun, now. As I watch, a blackbird stoops to drink.

Discovery – Creative Tension

Like most people in this culture, I spent the first forty years of my life seeing the world in terms of opposites: light and dark; war and peace; rain and shine; night and day; left wing/right wing; good guys versus bad guys. And like everybody else, I spent a lot of time trying to figure out winners and losers, right choices and wrong choices – and of course cheering for the good guys. (Which were the good guys, of course, was often a matter of opinion, since obviously the bad guys, too, thought they were good guys and so did everyone else on their team.)

All around me, there was evidence of another, deeper truth, and yet it took me forty years to see what it was. When I was seven, a doting relative gave me an electrical set. (Do they still make those? Probably not. I expect they are considered too dangerous.) It had a battery, wires, a little bell, a buzzer, a light bulb and various types of sockets. If you wired up the circuit correctly, you could make the bell ring, the buzzer buzz, the bulb light up. I loved it. I learned, by doing, the principles of electricity and how the positive charge and the negative charge work together to create the flow of energy along the wire. The penny didn't drop, though.

Neither did it drop when I learned to ride a bicycle. It never occurred to me that staying upright on a bicycle is an action which is actually composed of falling to the left, correcting the fall, falling to the right, correcting the fall, and so on. I was simply pleased that I could now ride without training wheels.

Steering a ship works the same way. I even had a go at steering an ocean liner once (courtesy of an indulgent captain who let me visit the bridge) but I still didn't get the message.

I would love to tell you a fascinating story about the moment when the penny finally did drop and I discovered that the point of opposites is not to eliminate one pole and award a laurel wreath to the other. I do remember the moment, and it was one of the great "aha" moments of my life. Yet I can't remember how it happened. All I can tell you is that I was listening to an old man with glasses and a flat cap, whose name I have forgotten. He was the friend of a friend who lived in a cabin in the mountains, and was making one of his rare visits to town. My friend took me to meet him, for a cup of tea and a chat, as she thought I might find him interesting. I cannot even remember what he said, but whatever it was, a huge light bulb went off in my head. In that moment, I suddenly saw clearly that all those pairs which we think of as opposites are actually pairs of life partners. For the whole world, just like my electric buzzer, is powered by the tension of opposites.

When a wire is stretched so tightly between two posts that the tension of trying to go both ways pulls it completely taut, a person can walk, dance and turn somersaults on it. The place between the two poles of a pair of opposites is the most creative place there is. An artist, caught between the tantalizing dance of his or her vision and the down to earth practicalities of brush and paint, strives to bring the two together. Usually, it never quite happens. If it did, and the artist painted the definitive picture, would s/he ever paint again? Probably not, for then the tension would be gone. The wire would go slack and the motivation cease. It is that creative tension between dream and materials which keeps the creativity constantly flowing and the canvases coming.

The most creative moments of our lives are not only when we are creating objects but when we are creating ourselves. The teenager, caught in a four-way pull between childhood and adulthood, and between family and peer group, creates the unique man or woman who will move out into the world. And at fifty or thereabouts, the tension between the conformity of those earlier, income-producing, family-making years and the beckoning freedom of the future enables many men and women to re-invent themselves in order to live every moment of their "third age" to the full.

Remember, too, how the most fertile places in the landscape are those where opposites meet and touch. The edge between the forest and the plain, the littoral, where ocean touches shore, is where you find the richest biodiversity of all. There are always many more birds on the edges of a wood than there are within the wood or beyond it.

The more I think about duality, the more I appreciate it in this new way. Deepening my understanding of creative tension has given me a completely new attitude towards those trade-offs which pop up at every turn.

Setting off for a long camping trip around the south-western desert areas of the USA, my partner and I faced the dilemma of wanting some cooked meals but not wanting to light fires (because of the drought and the scarcity of firewood) or to use a lot of bottled gas. That dilemma gave birth to our first solar cooker, made from cardboard cartons, newspaper, aluminium foil and a sheet of glass. It cooked all our meals for the trip and got passed on to a friend in Santa Fe, who went on using it for years in her garden.

The necessity of finding resolution to a trade-off dilemma is the mother of many inventions like that. It is also the mother of new discoveries, and of deeper learning. My dislike of killing creatures, when it comes hard up against my preference for not having every leaf in my veggie garden devoured by slugs and snails, has given rise to a long educational process about the ways of these pesky molluscs and any number of innovative solutions. It also keeps me alert to other people's new solutions. (I'm trying out yet another this year: copper-topped weed mats.)

The trade-off which has the most emotion in it for me, at the moment, is the one between the desire to limit my use of fossil fuels and the desire to see my grandchildren, who live on the other side of the ocean. One flight across the Atlantic and back uses up more than my "allowance" of fuel oil for a whole year. So to do it is to take more than my share of the world's non-renewable energy. Which means that someone, somewhere, gets less than a full share, and that's not fair. On the other hand, it is sad for me, and for my grandchildren, if we can never see each other and play and hug and read stories and do all the things grandmothers and grandchildren do. I could chafe against this dilemma, or I could mine it for all that it has to offer. I have chosen the latter path. The creative tension between these two opposing desires has created quite a lot of good stuff. In order to "afford" (oil-wise) the occasional plane trip, I don't run a car. Which means I walk, ride my bicycle, get exercise. Which means I catch the bus, chat to people on the way, travel slowly enough to enjoy the scenery, avoid car repairs and the stress of driving, and one fewer car on the road helps to ease road congestion and pollution. Seeing those children so infrequently has made me think of all kinds of alternative ways to keep our connection, with postcards, with photos, with e-mail, telephone, etc.

So nowadays, whenever I come up against another trade-off, I try to befriend it. I see it in terms of creative tension and what might be born from that fertile place where opposites meet.

Step 6
Doing it Together

I have been speaking, throughout these chapters, as though you, the reader, were an isolated individual with the liberty to change your lifestyle at will, in any way you choose, without reference to anyone else. But what if you live with other people? If you have a partner and/or children, how might they feel about all this? Even though small changes can be made without anyone noticing, it takes courage to make big changes (like relocation or a lowered income) that affect a whole family.

(Though if you do have a family, maybe that is even more reason to move towards a simpler life; children need simple lives even more than grown-ups do.)

My twin grandsons were fanatical about Thomas the Tank Engine so someone gave them an expensive toy. It was a huge, complex contraption which had to be set up by an adult, but when it was set up properly it was fascinating to watch. Thomas whizzed around the tracks, backed into a docking station, dumped a load of small, black balls into a wagon which went up in a lift and then dumped the balls into another train, and so on. Amazing. Some toy designer's "inner child" undoubtedly had great fun designing all that. But of course these children wanted to have fun too. The problem was that all they could do with this thing was watch it. The minute they tried to play with it, everything stopped: bits fell off; tracks collapsed; trains tipped up and the little black balls ran in all directions, including all the way under the sofa (to the delight of the cat). Ten minutes later, after everyone had scrambled around retrieving all the balls, the structure was back in place and off went the little trains again; for a few seconds, anyway. How long do you imagine a small child can stand and watch something like that without touching it? After a few repetitions of this, my daughter was appalled to hear herself saying: "Don't touch it, sweetheart; it might break again." Whereupon the craziness of the situation dawned on her. She silently vowed that once this so-called "toy" went back in its box, there it would stay.

But it wasn't that easy. The boys clamoured for it again. And their father, who loved being with them on weekends because he saw so little of them during the week, seemed perfectly happy to go through the rigmarole of setting it up, watching it fall apart and setting it up again. So from then on, it became "The Thomas game you play with Daddy on Sundays". The rest of the week, the boys played with their ordinary, simple versions of Thomas the Tank Engine; the endless, and endlessly inventive games of imagination which turned the coffee table into a goods yard, the backs of chairs into steep hills and the whole living room into a landscape. Those were games which never broke and fell apart. They were extensive, complex, creative, interesting, interactive, and essentially simple.

This is a stunningly accurate illustration of the simplicity paradox; standing and watching something is about the simplest thing you can do with it. All the complexity is in the contraption itself and in the designing, making, shipping and selling of it. However, children are not programmed by Nature for passive watching: they are programmed to interact with their world in every minute. They are programmed for the simplicity of doing things themselves rather than the simplicity of being passive consumers. The latter, they have to be taught. ("Don't touch it, sweetheart, it might break.") So if you are a parent, have you paused to consider the extent to which our modern culture is damaging its children?

Toys you can only press buttons on and watch; TV companions with whom you cannot interact; child care from early morning to evening while harried parents work; schools that cage young children like battery hens, force-feeding them the National Curriculum; homework that eats up free time; the constant pressure to achieve and compete; the backing up of adolescence further and further so that ten year old girls are trying desperately to look sexy – these are all part of twenty-first century living in the Western world. And all these things are stealing childhood away from our children. Our nation's children are getting obese on the food we feed them. And we are prescribing them anti-depressants in ever-increasing quantities. We are training them, at younger and younger ages, to be sick canaries too.

It is time to stop, to take stock, to feel our way forwards into something better, healthier, and simpler. So if you have children, consider simplifying for their sakes, even if not for your own.

Remember, though, that the change process often moves more slowly for families than for single individuals. Partners might not be equally ready to make changes. Needs might be different. Whereas my daughter was all set to take that new Thomas toy to the nearest tip, my son-in-law was content to keep it around for a while, despite its problematical nature. And he was able to make its collapsibility a part of the game. For him, all that mattered was that he was spending time with his sons and they were all enjoying each other's company.

We can all find ways of adapting to the dysfunctional nature of our culture that make life less stressful and more fun for ourselves, and for our children if we have them. We can simplify slowly, by degrees. And partners who are changing at different rates can still rub along happily together.

Does it bother you that other people in your wider circle – your parents, friends, colleagues, etc. – might scoff or disapprove when they see you making fundamental changes to the way you live? Are you afraid the path to simplicity may turn out to be a lonely one?

It can be, at first. As you know, our innate longing for safety and security means we can feel threatened by changes in others close to us. Any change in the ideas, beliefs, habits or lifestyle of a family member, friend or colleague can be disquieting. After all, if I need stability and familiarity and you are a part of my immediate environment, when you change, my little boat begins to rock and I start to feel insecure. Even if I don't directly request that you change back to the way you were in order to restore my sense of personal comfort, it is likely that my unspoken (maybe even unconscious) demand "change back!" will hang in the air between us, affecting many of our interactions. Think of a mother's pursed lips when her teenage daughter first announces that she is planning to move out of home and share a flat with friends. The mother's world is changing just a little too quickly for her comfort. She probably adapts, but whether that adaptation takes only a few seconds or ten years depends on the sort of person she is. Most of us have to work at adapting, for there are few of us who have perfected the art of flowing with the river of change. So it is important to remember that any changes you make for yourself are likely to disconcert, albeit temporarily, others in your close circle.

Do you differ, in essential ways, from many of the people with whom you share your time? Most of us have learned that we can live and work quite companionably in a family, a workspace or a community without sharing many of the core values of the other people there. That can feel lonely sometimes, especially if you have no partner, or if you have a partner who does not fully share those core values. But even if you are in an intimate relationship with someone totally compatible, it is likely (especially if you work full-time) that you spend many hours a day outside that cosy cocoon of sharing, in a world you may perceive as somewhat hostile to your ideas. After a while, that can make you feel like a bit of an alien.

In which case, let me assure you that your interest in the issues raised in this book – simplifying one's life, living at a slower pace, more in harmony with the environment and with one's own, essential nature – is shared by many more people than you realize.

In the words of Paul Ray and Sherry Anderson: "... if you hunger for a deep change in your life that moves you in the direction of less stress, more health, lower consumption, more spirituality, more respect for the earth and the diversity within and among the species that inhabit her, YOU ARE NOT ALONE. You are one of a growing number of people who want to see deep, integral change in the cultures that have evolved in industrialized nations."

Ray and Anderson, after extensive research, estimated that by the year 2000, people in this category – whom they call "Cultural Creatives" – numbered around fifty million in North America and eighty to ninety million in the European Union. That's a lot of "aliens"!

As they explained:

"... We want to make cultural creatives visible to each other. We want cultural creatives to realize that we are the isolated many, not the isolated few. We want to invite cultural creatives to find new ways to work and learn together."

"Cultural Creatives are redefining what success means, away from success at work and making a lot of money, toward a more soulful life focused on personal fulfillment, social conscience, creating a better future for everyone on the planet."

In other words, the sort of simple life we are talking about here.

Since you are reading this book, you are probably one of these cultural creatives. If you are not sure whether you fit the description, this list can give you an idea. Choose the statements that you agree with.

You are likely to be a Cultural Creative if you...

1. love Nature and are deeply concerned about its destruction.
2. are strongly aware of the problems of the whole planet (global warming, destruction of rainforests, overpopulation, lack of ecological sustainability, exploitation of people in poorer countries) and want to see more action on them, such as limiting economic growth.
3. would pay more taxes or pay more for consumer goods if you could know the money would go to clean up the environment and to stop global warming.
4. place a great deal of importance on developing and maintaining your relationships.
5. place a lot of value on helping other people and bringing out their unique gifts.
6. do volunteering for one or more good causes.
7. care intensely about both psychological and spiritual development.
8. see spirituality or religion as important in your life, but are concerned about the role of the Religious Right in politics.
9. want more equality for women at work, and more women leaders in business and politics.
10. are concerned about violence and abuse of women and children

around the world.

11. want our politics and government spending to put more emphasis on children's education and well-being, on rebuilding our neighbourhoods and communities, and on creating an ecologically sustainable future.

12. are unhappy with both the Left and the Right in politics, and want to find a new way that is not in the mushy middle.

13. tend to be somewhat optimistic about our future, and distrust the cynical and pessimistic view that is given by the media.

14. want to be involved in creating a new and better way of life in your country.

15. are concerned about what the big corporations are doing in the name of making more profits: downsizing, creating environmental problems, and exploiting poorer countries.

16. have your finances and spending under control, and are not concerned about overspending.

17. dislike all the emphasis in modern culture on success and "making it", on getting and spending, on wealth and luxury goods.

18. like people and places that are exotic and foreign, and like experiencing and learning about other ways of life.

If you said "yes" to all or most of those statements, you are almost certainly one of this huge, hidden band of people who are trying to create a peaceful, sustainable world instead of the tumultuous, dangerous, inequitable, unstable and unsustainable one we currently have.

So you may find it helpful to link up with others who are finding ways to simplify their lives and form a simplicity circle. Though these are increasingly popular in North America, they are harder to find in the UK, so the best way to find one may be to start one yourself. If you have no friends or acquaintances interested in these things, you could try putting a notice in your local post office, health food shop or local newspaper. I would be very surprised if no-one responded. Also, remember that if you have access to the Internet, you can join a discussion with people all over the world.

You and I and all the other millions of Cultural Creatives are part of what theologian Thomas Berry has dubbed "The Great

Work". It is the work of pulling our human civilization (and the rest of life on our planet) back from the brink of disaster.

In Thomas Berry, we see another thinker, like Karl-Henrik in Chapter 2, who has found a rule of thumb to help him distinguish good from bad, desirable from undesirable, sustainable from unsustainable. When he was a child, there was a meadow behind his house, full of flowers and birds. One of his most vivid memories is of being eleven years old, standing at the fence, looking across the stream into the meadow and thinking how beautiful it was. For the rest of his life, he has used the health of that meadow as a measuring stick. He realized that everything, in the larger world, impacts in some way on that meadow. Intensive farming practices will cause bird species to decline so that there will be fewer birds in his meadow, the water quality in the stream will be affected by runoff. Pollution and global warming will create flood and drought that will irrevocably alter his meadow. Anything and everything can be examined in the light of what its ultimate effect on the meadow (and others like it) might be. As he puts it:

"Whatever preserves and enhances this meadow in the natural cycles of its transformation is good; whatever opposes this meadow or negates it is not good. My life orientation is that simple. It is also that pervasive. It applies in economics and political orientation as well as in education and religion."

In certain Native American traditions, the rule of thumb has always been to consider the effects of all one's actions on one's descendants, seven generations into the future. How much more careful we might have been with our toxic waste if we had used that rule!

The trouble is, most people are too busy and preoccupied to think about these things and to make the connections. The Way of Least Resistance is so much easier, and so apparently simple. You call into the supermarket for a litre of milk – what could be simpler than that? Well, nothing, except that:

• the money you handed over at the till will finish up in the pockets of CEOs and shareholders thousands of miles away, while local shopkeepers are forced to close down.

• the cow who produced the milk has been turned into a machine, her health ruined and her life shortened by the demands for ever-increasing milk yields.

• the fields the cow lives in have been artificially fertilized to make the grass grow more quickly, depleting the soil of minerals in the long term.

• the need for fast-growing grass means there are no longer any wildflowers in the fields, which means fewer seeds for the birds, which means fewer birds.

• the farmer, who gets only a few pence for the milk, is desperately trying not to go broke, so he or she is putting pressure on the cows and the fields to yield more.

• the plastic bottle the milk comes in caused pollution in its manufacture and will now have to go to the landfill, where it will take hundreds of years to break down again.

There's more. And that's just one litre of milk.

The Way of Consciousness involves joining up all those dots. So this is the huge paradox of trying to live a simple life. You take back on to yourself the responsibility for joining all the dots that most people do not bother to join. At first, that seems like a huge task. But, like learning to drive a car, once you have mastered it, it becomes second nature.

Once you have found all the alternatives that are right for you (the ways to live which, although they may seem less simple in the short term, are healthier in the long term for both you and the planet), living simply will be as natural and as easy as breathing. Your simple meal of fresh, organic vegetables, free range eggs, homemade bread and apple juice from the farmer's market will not only taste a hundred times more delicious than the "heat 'n' eat" concoction from the supermarket via the microwave, but you will know that it has caused no harm to your grandchildren's grandchildren's grandchildren's children, or to Thomas Berry's meadow or to the cells of your body, or to the planet on which we all live. And you will have time to relax as you eat it and to savour every mouthful. That's the simple life.

Lilypad Principle 6
We All Make A Difference
Being the change you want to see

An awful lot seems to have gone wrong with our world in the last fifty years. In fact, the process has been going on much longer than that, but, like the frogs in the pot, no-one noticed for a long, long time just how much was wrong, so it feels more sudden than it really is. It is no good blaming anyone though. Remember, we all do the best we can.

When DDT was first made, everyone genuinely thought it was a wonderful invention. Including me. I remember spraying cockroaches with it back in the early 1950s. Nobody realized, in the beginning, the havoc it would cause. Mistakes only become mistakes when we have the benefit of hindsight.

It is important to look back and see what has gone wrong and why and how, so that we don't repeat history. Nevertheless, it can be overwhelming, once we see the enormity of the problem. That is when we are likely to throw our hands up in despair and say "But what can I do? I am only one person."

It is interesting, however, that at the same time we are realizing the extent of environmental and social devastation on our planet we are also connecting with each other on a global basis like never before, especially via the Internet. More and more people are linking up, mobilizing, calling for change, creating change, inspiring and encouraging one another.

To me, Gandhi's dictum, *Be the change you want to see happen in the world,* is one of the most empowering sentences ever spoken. Because we are all connected and because we know, from quantum physics, that even a small change that happens in one place is inevitably going to have a ripple effect, then even the tiniest change you make towards a simpler way of living will have all manner of effects on other people, in other places – effects which you cannot even begin to predict.

All you have to do, therefore, is to relax, open all your senses, live in the fullness and completeness of each present moment, make choices based on what is best for Thomas Berry's meadow, for seven generations of your descendants and (at the most fundamental level of all) for the living cell. There is plenty more you can do if you wish – enough to keep all the activists on Earth busy twenty-four hours a day. But there is no more that you need to do to be part of the solution rather than part of the problem. Living simply is enough. If everyone did it, the problems would be over.

Chapter Seven

"Ice"

The trees are bare. A cold, north wind finds its way in to the bare skin at the back of my neck, and I turn up my collar. Fingers wrapped around the bunch of kale I have just picked for our dinner are already numb with cold.

But instead of hurrying back to the kitchen's warm comfort, I walk a few steps further up the garden. I like to look at my little pond, even when there's nothing happening in it – at least, nothing that my human eyes can discern.

There has been ice on the surface since the day before yesterday, when the mercury dropped to freezing point and stayed there.

I reach over and tap it. It is such a thin film that it bends downwards and breaks, and brown water with its green blobs of duckweed hurries to fill the gap.

What do those dark, brown depths conceal now? Did a toad find that flower pot and decide to overwinter there, as I had hoped?

Life in the garden has slowed to a quiet ticking-over. Even the winter greens – the kale, the spinach, the bok choy – grow so slowly that we have to be careful our appetites do not overtake them. Those weeds which were so virile and rampant all summer have either scattered their seeds, turned brown and died or, as in the case of the ever-persistent buttercups, they have dozed off, content to wait out this time of cold, short days and scarce sunlight.

Wherever the frogs are, they are asleep too, their body rhythms slowed, their slow-moving blood the same temperature as the surrounding stones.

I found a small lizard on my morning walk yesterday. It was sitting at the edge of the road, not moving. At first, I thought it was dead. But it was breathing. I picked it up and it did not resist. It was a limp, cold thing, unable to do more than slowly, feebly wave one leg a little. How it got into the road, I have no idea. But it obviously had no energy to move itself to safety.

I put it in my pocket and continued my walk. When I got home, I came up here to a place just across from the pond where I had secreted a section of pipe in amongst some rocks and placed some hay inside it. I had hoped that some reptile in search of real estate would discover this choice location, but so far none had. It would, I thought, make a perfect home for my new friend.

When I reached into my pocket, the lizard was now wide awake and very lively. The warmth of my body had brought its energy back in full force and I could scarcely hold it for the wriggling. When I placed it at the doorway of the pipe, it scampered eagerly in. I wonder if it is still there. Or did it squander the energy it borrowed from my body by going in search of further adventures, while it still could? I resist the temptation to poke around in the pipe and see if it is still there. This is a time for patience. A time for trusting. When the right time comes, the seeds will germinate, the garden will glow green again, the pace of life will quicken once more. And the frogs will return.

As I walk back indoors I reflect how good it feels, at some deep, primal level I cannot explain, to live so simply and consciously according to the seasons. Right now I am adapting my activities to the slow rhythms and long nights of winter. I sleep longer. I write, I read, I take inner journeys. I stay home more, snug inside this little cottage which feels a lot like a cave, only much, much cosier. I let my own sap subside, and tune into the slow, quiet pulse of the Earth. There is something hugely satisfying about that.

Discovery – Simplicity and Synchronicity

The seventh discovery I want to share with you is that there is a clear connection between simplicity and synchronicity.

"Synchronicity," as you probably know, is a term coined by psychiatrist C.G. Jung to describe the apparent coincidences which arise when people start using their intuitive sense.

The intuitive or "sixth" sense has been the Cinderella of the senses in our techno-crazy, super-rational Western culture. But despite that, and despite its being seen as something possessed only by women, there are many well-known stories which show that many, probably most, of the great discoveries in science have come (to men as often as to women) by way of pure intuition.

Nowadays, there appears to be a growing awareness of how important intuition is to us. Books, courses, videos, instruction manuals abound, exhorting us to awaken this dormant sense – as though there were something mysterious, something arcane and difficult, about using an ability which is in fact as natural to us as breathing.

Like breathing, if we focus on it, it suddenly feels forced, strange, awkward. So I doubt we can learn much about this sixth sense by putting it in the spotlight of our conscious awareness. That is a light too bright. Intuition is a programme that runs quietly in the background. And what I have discovered is that the trick to developing it is simply to relax and to trust it completely, like we do with our breathing.

The simple life, because it is quieter, more peaceful, slower, and less stressful than the usual, mainstream life, gives us many more opportunities to hear the quiet voice of intuition. When our minds are uncluttered, it is easier to notice our first response – the gut response or the heart response – to things, before our rational minds come booming in to drown out its gentle sound. And when we catch that first response, there is time to turn up the volume, to let ourselves become fully aware of what our hearts and guts are trying to say, rather than hurriedly tuning them out and then losing the message. For lost messages, if they are important, can shape-shift into something like procrastination or even a headache or irritable bowel in their attempt to be heard.

Remember the earlier chapter in this book which spoke of signposts? At that point, we were looking for things which had already settled into our lives: the headaches, the "bad habits" which were the result of ignoring our sixth sense way back when. What we are doing now is figuring out how to pre-empt those happenings, to learn how to stop them before they start.

There is no mystery about intuition. It is simply our felt sense of connection with the rest of the Earth, our tuning in to that place where nothing is separate from anything else.

I remember the first time I went to visit my daughter after she moved to Boston, Massachusetts. I had been staying in her apartment for the weekend, and on Monday she had to work. But we had arranged to meet in the foyer of the large, downtown building where she worked and go to lunch together. She wrote down the address on a piece of paper, and gave me a city map. I put both in my pocket without looking at them. I had never been to the downtown area before, though I had seen the roofs of its buildings clustering together on the far side of Boston Common, so I thought it would be fun to set off early and do some exploring.

It was a glorious day, and I love to walk. So I headed across the Common, enjoying the scenery, the weather, the sights and sounds all around me. There was plenty of time. I looked forward with great anticipation to seeing my daughter, who I love so dearly and whose company I so much enjoy. Once I reached the downtown area, I wandered happily around without noticing street names. I had no idea where I was. After a while, I saw that it was getting towards the time we had arranged to meet. I waited at a traffic light, thinking that after I crossed the intersection I would take out the piece of paper and the map, see where I was, then find my way to the meeting place. But even as I crossed the road I knew, intuitively, that the building immediately ahead of me was the one where my daughter worked. Sure enough, it was. That is synchronicity. It looks like coincidence, but it is not. The combination of my deep connectedness with my daughter, my relaxed, happy, unstressed mood, and our intention to meet had drawn me unerringly to the exact right spot, just as a salmon finds its way upriver to its spawning ground. The process always works, if we let it; the trick is to relax enough to allow it.

As I have relaxed more and more into the simple life, these synchronicities have been happening with ever greater frequency, so much so that they have become a barometer. If none happen for a while, it is a sign that I have wandered off course a little and need to remind myself of the Lilypad List of simplicity principles: avoiding self-blame; taking time out; cultivating silence; staying closely attuned to my senses; honouring my body; trusting the process instead of seeking certainty; remembering that everything is connected; and living as much as I can in the "now moment". Whenever I can do all that, everything clicks back into place, my intuition works effortlessly and synchronicities happen.

It's a bit like getting gold stars for good behaviour!

Step 7

Just Doing It

I have shared with you the small stories of my frog pond and some of the travel tales from my (still ongoing) spiral journey towards the simple life. I have shared my key discoveries, and I have asked you a lot of questions.

I have suggested where you might seek clues to the changes you could make. And I have given you some ideas, some foundations upon which to build a life that's simpler, sweeter and more fulfilling than the one you have been leading up till now. I have tried to do all this without driving you to despair over the ecological and social justice problems of our beleaguered planet, and to remind you that you can, indeed, make a difference to those, simply by living simply.

There are more tools, at the end of this book, which you can use to guide you on your journey: books to read; a self-therapy technique to use for peering more deeply into the corners of your unconscious mind; and a tape measure to estimate the size of your ecological footprint.

By now, I hope that the blueprint for your new, simpler life has started to take shape in your mind.

All that remains is doing it.

Some people do not choose simplicity; they get plunged into it when life events cause a sudden drop in income or a restriction on mobility. Things like bereavement, divorce, getting sacked or laid off, illness or a collapse in the stock market can all force people into a drastically pared-down lifestyle which they may not have planned for at all. Starting into it that way is a bit like the situation where the only way you can start your car is by rolling it down a steep hill, which is not something most of us would normally choose to do.

Although they struggle with it and resent it at the time, people forced into a simpler lifestyle by circumstances sometimes look back later and see the precipitating crisis as a blessing. They end up feeling grateful to whatever event it was that dislodged them from their previous comfort zone. Not always, but very often.

People who lose all or most of their possessions through fire or other disaster often report that, after the initial period of shock and grief passed, an unexpected feeling of freedom and lightness emerged – a delight in the simplicity of owning next to nothing. When a friend's house was ransacked by a burglar and everything of value taken, she felt devastated. But she told me later that the insurance money had enabled her to replace the large amount of stuff she had lost with just a few, high quality items that better reflected the person she now was. Like a snake which had shed its skin, losing her lifetime's accumulation of objects enabled her to create a better fit between the material world and her changing, evolving self.

I am not suggesting that we all need crisis to catapult us into simpler ways of living. But most of us need something with which to start the transition. What I recommend is a "Time-out experience", or TOE for short. (I like that acronym, as it has connotations of putting one's toe in the water.)

TOEs tend to happen of their own accord, anyway. Whenever visitors from the city arrived at the retreat centre we were building in the foothills of the Australian Alps, they invariably had a spontaneous TOE.

When they first arrived, we could feel the city vibes humming through them. They leaped out of their cars, gulping huge lungfuls of our clean air, excited to be there, eager to help with the mudbrick making or the gardening and saying things like: "Give me a spade – set me to work!"

To which we replied: "We don't let visitors work on their first day. Just relax and enjoy being here."

If it was still early in the day, I could guarantee that they would disappear straight after lunch and turn up again hours later, rubbing their eyes and apologizing for sleeping all afternoon. "I only lay down for a little rest. Didn't mean to go to sleep."

By nine p.m. on that first day, they would have succumbed again. It was the same pattern again next day. "I don't know what is the matter with me," they would say. "All I seem to want to do is sleep!"

"That's just the way it should be," we would assure them. "You are just soaking all the accumulated stress and tiredness out of your bones."

Sure enough, by the third or fourth day, they would be full of energy again. But it was a different kind of energy – a peaceful, simple energy that resonated with their surroundings.

Then, of course, they were reluctant to go home. Once you have touched into that simplicity space, you want to stay there. That's precisely why TOEs are so beneficial for anyone interested in simplifying his or her lifestyle.

Most people who go on a retreat report that their minds and bodies take time to adjust to the slow pace of life and the lack of outside stimulation. Sometimes they feel churned up for a while, as all the things they have been pushing out of their minds come rushing back in. But gradually, as they relax into this new, slower rhythm, a feeling of joyfulness starts bubbling up. Simple things, like the scent of honeysuckle or the song of a bird outside the window, now seem incredibly sweet and beautiful.

So creating some kind of TOE for yourself is the best way to start your new life. If you can find that place of sweetness, that quiet, fertile place, then you will be much more able to implement the practices I have talked about in this book – the practices which will give you the infrastructure for living simply and savouring every moment of it. These are the practices of staying in tune with your animal senses and your hunter-gatherer body, cultivating the witness-self and staying in the "now" (both of which I shall be talking about next) and trusting the process.

Yes, you can create the physical infrastructure by emptying out your attic, trading your fancy, petrol-guzzling car for a smaller, eco-friendlier one, downsizing to a smaller living space, recycling everything, wearing second-hand clothes and all the rest of it. But only when your mind has moved into a different gear will you start to feel the delight bubbling up – delight in your surroundings, delight in simple pleasures, delight in just breathing and being alive.

There is an old, Zen teaching story that I love to tell. It is (like most Zen stories) about a student who wanted to study with a famous master. In this case, the master presented the would-be student with a fish in a tank. "Go and study this fish and come back when you know all there is to know about it," he said.

The student took the fish to his room and began diligently studying it. He measured the fish, noted its colours and patterns, the arrangement of its scales and fins, the way it moved, the way it opened and closed its mouth, and so on. He wrote it all down carefully in his notebook. When he had finished, he took the fish and notebook to the master and read out all that he had learned.

The master's only response was to hand him back the fish. "Go and study the fish," he said. "You are not ready to work with me until you know all about this fish."

Crestfallen, the student carried the tank back to his room and sat down, despondently staring at the fish. After a while, he remembered that he had not counted its teeth. That took a while, but he managed it. He also found a few other things about the fish that he had previously overlooked and noted those down. He waited a day, but could think of no other observations to make. So back he went.

The master dismissed him with an impatient wave of the hand. "Just go and study your fish."

This happened several more times. Each time, the poor student returned to his quarters, lugging the fish tank. By now, he was alternating between rage and despair. He hated the master, he hated the fish. He wanted to go home. But this was a highly respected Zen master, a once-in-a-lifetime opportunity. He didn't want to be a quitter.

So he decided just to sit with his feelings for a while. (And with the fish.) He began to notice his own thoughts. After many hours, he reached the point where he could discern even the tiniest beginnings of thoughts. He also started noticing very subtle aspects of the fish that he hadn't been aware of before. The longer he sat and the quieter he became, the more he noticed.

Hours, days, weeks went by. The student had become so absorbed in all the subtleties he was observing about himself and about the fish that he lost track of time. The longer it went on, the more fascinating it was. By now, he was in love with the fish, in love with the process, in love with life.

One day, the master walked past the open door of the student's room and saw him sitting there, in rapt observation of the fish in the tank. "Come on," he said. "Bring back that fish. We'll start work now."

Like the Zen student and like the visitors to our mountain retreat, it is unlikely that you can go immediately from where you are to where you want to be. Like them, you probably need a TOE in order to shift to that other gear.

Seen from the outside – from the perspective of a typical, consumerist/materialist, mainstream lifestyle, full of buzz and busyness, sensation and stimulation and the endless grasping for an illusory security – the simple life can look dull, boring and insufficient to keep a person happy, which is probably why so many people say they want it and even read books about it but never really make the switch.

The Zen student had to struggle before he made that switch and was able to drop into the new space. The retreat visitors just had to rest and withdraw for a while. Some people have to experience a bit of both. Struggle and withdrawal can both be part of a TOE. Either way, if you want to drop into that place where what appeared empty suddenly becomes full to overflowing and simple pleasures become rich sources of delight, create a TOE for yourself.

If being forced by circumstances into simplifying your life is like rolling your car downhill to start it, then a TOE is like having a starter motor. This book, and others like it, are like the battery that supplies the initial current. You cannot run your car just with a battery. Books and articles on simple living, though you may find them encouraging, even inspiring, cannot of themselves get your engine going. Only you can do that, out of the conviction that comes from having sampled simplicity in one or more of its forms and having acquired a taste for it. Once you have done that, the process is self-perpetuating.

So here are some suggestions for creating a TOE for yourself:

- Go on a one-week media fast: no TV, no newspapers, no magazines.
- Take time off work and go on retreat. You can either go to a retreat centre, create a retreat-style holiday or design your own retreat at home.
- Go on a pilgrimage of some kind, or a long-distance walk.

There are more suggestions on the Lilypad List website: www.lilypadlist.com

A Word of Warning

It is not the *content* of our lives which defines them as simple, but the *process*. A Japanese diner outside a seafood restaurant, an anxious patient in a psychiatrist's waiting room and a marine biology student in an aquarium might each be staring intently at a fish in a tank. But they are probably not seeing it the way the Zen student was seeing his when the master paused in the doorway. The inside, not the outside, is what counts. Mindset, attitude, the quality of attention – they are everything.

Don't listen to anyone who tells you that something you are doing or having or enjoying is not appropriate because you are "supposed" to be living simply. People are often surprised when they discover that I have three hundred and fifty different versions of solitaire on my computer and love to play them. "Wouldn't a pack of cards be more appropriate for someone like you who is committed to the simplicity lifestyle?", they ask me.

That's when I know they have missed the point.

Lilypad Principle 7
There is Only the Now Moment
Cultivating the skill of mindfulness

Much of the time, our minds keep themselves (or rather, us) busy, holding either post-mortems on past moments or rehearsals for future ones. Like restless monkeys, they rarely settle peacefully in the only moment that matters: this one.

There are times, however, when whatever we are doing holds our attention so fully and completely that the "now" moment expands and we are held for a while in timelessness. Psychologist, Mihaly Csikszentmihalyi (in case you want to read this aloud, it's pronounced "me high, chicks send me high"), has made a lifelong study of this. He calls it The Flow Phenomenon.

This is how Csikszentmihalyi describes the feeling of being "in the flow":

1. You are completely involved in the activity, focused, concentrating – with this either due to innate curiosity or as the result of training.
2. There is a sense of ecstasy, of being outside everyday reality. You experience great inner clarity, knowing what needs to be done and how well it is going.
3. You have a strong knowing that the activity is do-able – that your skills are adequate, so there is neither anxiety nor boredom.
4. You feel a sense of serenity – no worries about self, feeling of growing beyond the boundaries of ego – afterwards and a feeling of transcending ego in ways not thought possible.
5. There is a timelessness about it; you are thoroughly focused on the present, and don't notice time passing.
6. There is an intrinsic motivation in all this – i.e. whatever produces "flow" in you becomes its own reward, so you continue the activity in order to continue having the feeling.

We have all experienced this at times. Sportspeople call it "The Zone" and strive to get there, knowing that their best performance happens in that space. Musicians, artists, all creative people know it well. The most fortunate among us are those who can reach the Flow state in the course of their everyday work and activities, rather than having to go rock climbing on weekends to achieve it. (Flow is the state our Zen student was in by the end of the story.)

You will no doubt recognize this state and know what is most likely to produce it for you.

Csikszentmihalyi's research has shown that spending time in the Flow state is good for one's health, for life satisfaction and a host of other desirable things. While it is not necessarily true that only morally good actions produce Flow (safebreakers , for example, probably experience it when they are absorbed in the feel and sound of those tumblers), it is likely that many of the activities which produce it in you are benign and desirable ones. So part of your program of simplifying may be to try and incorporate as many of these activities into your life as you can.

I have found that even when activities themselves do not anchor me in the "now" moment, I can keep myself there by the deliberate practise of mindfulness. This is achieved by developing the "witness self", a non-judging, non-interfering, purely observing "me" which comments objectively on whatever thoughts, feelings, actions, etc. are occupying my mind-space in any given moment. It is a technique best developed in the context of meditation, which can then be gradually extended to encompass more and more of everyday life.

I find that the more I anchor my moment-by-moment awareness in my senses, the easier it is to notice the mental processes, the thoughts and feelings which come flickering across my mental screen like so many TV commercials, tempting me to buy their products. Once I notice them, I am free to follow them or not, as I choose.

If I do not watch them in this way, my thoughts and feelings become the inner herons which snatch me from the stillness of my simple life. So this practise of mindfulness is a key one for our purposes here.

There are many excellent books and teachers of mindfulness, for not only is it a practice which you will find at the heart of all the world's great wisdom traditions – Buddhism, Christianity, Judaism, the Sufi traditions of Islam, the Vedanta of India, and so on – but it has also burst on to the "Mind Body Spirit" scene in recent times, following the publication of Eckhart Tolle's popular book, *The Power of Now* (which, by the way, I highly recommend). Any one of these teachers can explain the concepts and practices much better than I can. Especially Tolle. As he says:

"Die to the past every moment. You don't need it. Only refer to it when it is absolutely relevant to the present. Feel the power of this moment and the fullness of Being. Feel your presence."

All I can add is that whenever you are able to stay in the now, like that, living a simple life becomes the simplest task you could ever imagine.

Ending

Nuts and Bolts:
Practicalities of the Simple Life

Rather than supplying prescriptions for living simply, the aim of this book has been to enable you to create your own, unique prescription.

Nevertheless, before we part, I want to say a little about the many practical forms which "the simple life" may take, and to point out some resources which you may find useful.

I am aware that my personal version of simple living is not widely applicable, since my children are all grown up and my partner and I are retired, with no further need to earn our living. However, managing comfortably as we do on the meagre pensions paid to us by the State, we are proof that it is not necessary (as so many financial counsellors insist) to save hundreds of thousands in order to live well in retirement.

Some of the ingredients in my own simplicity recipe are:
– cutting possessions to a minimum and following the "one thing: many uses" principle
– living in a very small house
– living without a car, TV, washing machine, dishwasher, or microwave
– growing much of my own food (organically) and saving seeds
– living as much as possible within my local economy
– travelling on foot, by bicycle or on public transport wherever possible
– composting, recycling, repairing, re-using, buying things second-hand
– using low-energy light-bulbs
– using eco-friendly personal care and cleaning products
– preparing simple meals from basic, healthy ingredients and eating what is in season
– exercising, meditating, sleeping eight hours a night, eating and drinking healthily
– walking several miles a day and using the "Earth Gym"
– avoiding addictive substances (including sugar and coffee)

– reading the news online instead of buying newspapers
– paying bills by direct debit
– avoiding disposable products, e.g. paper towels, paper cups, tin-foil, gift-wrap
– using barter and LETS (local currency systems) to exchange some goods and services
– making my own greeting cards and recycling all envelopes
– banking with ethical banks
– refusing plastic bags and unnecessary packaging
– using herbal or homeopathic remedies instead of drugs

There are many other possible ingredients, and your "recipe" may turn out looking very different from mine. However, it can be helpful to read other people's recipes, to get ideas.

As you probably know, much has been written on the topic, especially in the last decade or so since "downshifting" became trendy and "simplicity" became a buzz-word. When it is all put together, it makes a huge, patchwork quilt, with all the pieces contributing colour, variety and usefulness to the whole. (I hope this book will form another useful square.)

Most simplicity books originate from the USA and are written primarily for North American readers. Whilst the issues that we have been discussing are universal and the seven steps I have outlined are relevant for anyone living in the so-called Western world, when it comes to the practicalities of living simply there are some important differences between the North American lifestyle and that of Europeans. Because of these key differences, books on the practical aspects of simple living do not always translate well between continents.

In the UK, we have a centuries-old infrastructure of settlement which, despite the vast changes of recent years (particularly the huge rise in car travel, the building of motorways and the proliferation of shopping malls and supermarkets), make it possible to live very simply. Many, probably most, of the people in my own, small, rural community now own cars and drive fifteen miles to the supermarket for their weekly shopping. Yet it is still possible for me to live without a car, take a bus to town, and buy my groceries in local and High Street shops and markets. The ancient infrastructure of small roads and lanes, local buses, village shops and Post Offices, local markets, etc., though badly eroded in recent decades, does still exist. I can walk or cycle safely, find my way by bus, train or ferry to any part of the British Isles (or, come to that, any part of Europe). The old infrastructure enables me, and others like me, to live simply and inexpensively but well. Furthermore, the more people who live this way, the sooner this structure will become revitalized. The more people spend their money locally instead of letting it be siphoned off by multinational corporations, the better our local communities, with all their wonderful, regional diversity, will prosper. When local economies prosper, small farmers and smallholders retain their livelihoods and the countryside retains its vitality and authenticity, rather than becoming a theme park for tourists.

The same goes for all the countries of Europe, each of which has its own traditional, folk culture. In all these countries those ancient cultures, which in every case have been an essential part of their fabric, are being threatened by the spread of global capitalism, as it gradually re-flavours the whole world plain vanilla. But in each of these places, those who are using the traditional infrastructures in order to live simply are helping to keep them alive.

Another factor is that here in the UK we have a National Health Service which, cumbersome and imperfect though it is, enables us to live, if we wish to, without the crippling expense of health insurance.

In the USA and Canada the story is very different and people on very low incomes are far more vulnerable. There, the sorts of infrastructures we have here in Europe simply do not exist. So, in North America, to live in a rural area without a car and to shop locally, both of which I do here, is a difficult challenge. In one part of the US where I lived for a while, it was a fifty-two mile round trip by car to the nearest grocery store, which was part of a chain. The town it was in had no sidewalks. The banks all had "drive-up" windows, as did the eating places (which were all fast-food outlets except for one Chinese restaurant); even the mailboxes were "drive-up".

I did live simply there, but only because at that time I was part of an intentional community, in which all the resources were shared. This solution works for many people. Intentional communities, co-housing settlements and "eco-villages" are becoming increasingly popular and numerous. Living co-operatively is the most sustainable way of all, so this trend is a bright hope for the future.

Ironically, living my version of the simple life in the USA was also easy when I lived right in the heart of downtown San Francisco, where everyone walks, public transport is plentiful, local shops abound, there is a farmers' market, and owning a vehicle is more a liability than an asset. But city rents are high, so it cannot be done on a very low income.

In outback Australia, where rural living may result in being not just twenty-six miles from a shop but several hundred, and where a car may be less useful than a light aircraft, my comments on practicalities may have even less relevance. Though once again, for city-dwellers, the differences are minimal.

Despite the difficulties I have mentioned, there is a huge amount of interest in simple living in North America, especially since the mid-1990s. The epicentre of this is the Pacific Northwest, but there are people all over the continent meeting in simplicity circles, supporting each other's efforts to simplify their lives and spreading their ideas ever more widely. Most books and websites on the subject originate from there.

I have divided the books into ten categories. In each category I have picked out one or more that I consider the most useful. I hope that you will find this a helpful tool.

You will notice that I have not included Internet resources here. That is because electronic resources shift and change and some of the URLs I might give you might be out of date before this book is out of print.

However, there are some extremely useful resources online so my way of making these available to you is the dedicated website – www.lilypadlist.com – which I intend to keep current for as long as this book remains in print (or as long as I, myself, remain "in print" – whichever applies!). On that, you will find a current list of useful online resources. If you have an Internet connection, I hope you will visit.

Now to the books: happy browsing!

Category 1.
Sharing resources: Eco-villages, co-housing, communal living

Recommended title:
Creating a Life Together
By Diana Leafe Christian

Anyone contemplating setting up, or moving into, any of these communal-living situations would benefit from this book of hard-nosed, practical advice, based on the combined experience and wisdom of many people who learned these things the hard way. Forget woolly, romantic fantasies about communal living and substitute the sort of careful, skilful preparation that Christian so sensibly advocates.

Anyone who grew up in a nuclear family (i.e. most of us) has a lot to learn, and unlearn, when making this kind of move. But the rewards are great, especially for families with children, and living communally in some form or another is a wonderful way to bring your ecological footprint way down.

Category 2. Frugality/Ethical Investment

Recommended title:
Your Money or Your Life: Transforming Your Relationship with Money & Achieving Financial Independence
By Joe Dominguez & Vicki Robin

No-one has ever tried to improve on this definitive book in the financial simplicity category. Its step-by-step program to financial independence has helped thousands of people simplify their lifestyle and dramatically change their relationship with money. Vicki Robin and the late Joe Dominguez took back their lives by gaining control of their money. They both gave up successful, and stressful, careers

in order to live more deliberately and meaningfully. Their book shows you how to:
- get out of debt and develop savings
- re-order material priorities and live well on less
- resolve inner conflicts between values and lifestyles
- convert problems into opportunities to learn new skills
- attain a wholeness of livelihood and lifestyle
- save the planet while saving money
- and much more

Category 3. De-cluttering

Recommended title:
Clutter's Last Stand: It's Time to De-Junk Your Life
By Don Aslett

This is by far the best book I have read on getting rid of clutter. And certainly the funniest. It is the only one which ever really worked for me; I had always been a hoarder, until I read it. After which, I laughed all the way to Oxfam, loaded down with bulging garbage bags.

Aslett takes no prisoners. Read it, and all the excuses you have ever had for hanging on to anything you neither adore nor regularly use will blow away like barley husks in the stiff breeze of his logic.

Apart from the humour, though, the best thing about Aslett's book is the solid connections he makes between stress of many kinds and the outward accumulation of "stuff". He shows how, by trimming the clutter from our lives, we can live so much more joyfully and feel more light and free than we could ever have imagined.

Category 4. Downshifting

(See also: "General Simplicity Handbooks")

("Downshifters" are folk who have achieved a good measure of material success and then have chosen to drop out of the "fast lane", either to take early retirement or to scale down to part-time work, work from home, consulting, etc. I have therefore put it in a category of its own, apart from the general "How to simplify" titles.)

Recommended title:
Downshifting: The Guide to Happier, Simpler Living
By Polly Ghazi & Judy Jones

I have chosen this one (a) because it is comprehensive and well written and (b) because it is one of the few books on the topic published here in UK.

Both successful Fleet Street journalists, Polly and Judy took voluntary redundancy packages in 1996 in order to, as they put it, "get a life". In 1997, noting that the downshifting trend (i.e. the trend towards working fewer hours for less pay and moving to a simpler, more frugal lifestyle) was gaining momentum in the USA, they predicted that the same would happen in the UK. So they published this self-help book for an English readership, based on their own experiences and research. It is an excellent, practical, wide-ranging guidebook for anyone who is planning to downshift, or contemplating such a move. Here's a quote:

"In the euphoria of post-World War II economic and technological advance, we came to despise almost anything that was from an earlier era, whether it was a piece of furniture or a set of values. We wanted to throw it out, and replace it with something a bit more modern. Consumption became the thing: a refrigerator, a front-loading washing machine, a TV set for the sitting-room, a nice car for trips at the weekend. All mod cons: that's what we wanted. We aren't so sure now whether the twin gods of capitalism and rampant consumerism have landed us quite where we want to be. Perhaps more than ever before, we are wondering what life is all about, what it's for. We are searching for meaning and balance. Many are turning to alternative ways of living, and downshifting is one of them. Indeed, in Western societies downshifting is one of the fastest developing social trends of the late 1990s, as more of us yearn for simpler, more fulfilling lives and the time to enjoy the good things in life."

Category 5. Mindfulness/Living in the Now

Recommended title:
The Buddhist Path to Simplicity: Spiritual Practice for Everyday Life
By Christina Feldman

Feldman points out that the key to living simply is a spiritual one. All we need to do to create a life of totally satisfying simplicity is to learn to live in the present moment and nowhere else:

"We do not have to travel far to discover simplicity. Each encounter, event and moment is a mirror that reflects our reactions, fears, longings and stories... The present moment we are in offers everything we need to discover the deepest serenity and most profound simplicity. There is not a better moment, a more perfect moment for us to awaken and uncover the immediacy and well-being we long for."

"Simplicity will not be found in trying to mold life to comply with our desires and expectations. The events and circumstances of our world feel no obligation to conform to our expectations. Again and again we learn that the gap between what is and what "should be" is an ocean of distress, disappointment and frustration. These feelings are not intrinsic to living but derive from our unwillingness to turn our hearts and minds to the realities of each moment. To have the wisdom to acknowledge the bare truths of the moment – "this is grief", "this is fear", "this is frustration" – enables us to lay down the burden of our stories and "shoulds," and follow the road to peace. Simplicity is born of a depth of understanding that enables us to harmonize our inner world with the changes and unpredictability of life."

Easier said than done, of course, and millions of spiritual seekers the world over are engaged for their whole lifetimes in just this one, simple practice. But there is no better spiritual path to follow.

Two other authors whose work I have found to be the most useful in this regard, though not specifically geared to the simplicity-seeker, are Charlotte Joko Beck and Eckhardt Tolle (see Bibliography).

Category 6. Studies of People Living Simply

I have included three titles here, partly because I think we benefit greatly from hearing each other's stories and partly because these three books are very different:

Living Lightly: Travels in Post-Consumer Society
By Walter and Dorothy Schwarz

A fascinating account by an English couple of how people around the world are adjusting their lifestyles to reduce their impact on the natural environment and achieve a more socially sustainable way of life.

Ordinary People as Monks and Mystics: Lifestyles for Self-Discovery
By Marsha Sinetar

What makes an individual separate him or herself out from the crowd and start walking to a different drumbeat?

Marsha Sinetar (author of *Do What You Love and the Money Will Follow*) is fascinated by those who opt out of the mainstream culture and create lifestyles that are more satisfying, sustainable, creative and in harmony with the Earth. Who are these people, and what do they have in common?

Her research shows that they can be found everywhere, in city apartments as well as in rural retreats. They are all highly individual, but they do have certain common features, features which, as Sinetar points out, show interesting similarities to the monks of the Middle Ages and the mystics of all the great spiritual traditions.

An interesting and unusual book.

Choosing Simplicity: Real People Finding Peace and Fulfilment in a Complex World
By Linda Breen Pierce

This is a big book, based on several years of research into the people and lifestyles of what Duane Elgin, the "father" of the simplicity movement, called "voluntary simplicity". A wonderful compendium of stories and characters.

Category 7. Simplicity Circles

Recommended Title:
Circle of Simplicity: Return to the Good Life
By Cecile Andrews

Cecile is the inspiration behind simplicity circles in North America. Here she shares her ideas and her personal stories.

Category 8. General Simplicity Handbooks
(see also "Downshifting")

Recommended: two titles, both US-based, but both really comprehensive:

The Simple Living Guide: A Sourcebook for Less Stressful, More Joyful Living
By Janet Luhrs

A "downshifter" herself, Janet Luhrs is one of the foremost experts on the topic and is editor and publisher of *Simple Living: The Journal of Voluntary Simplicity*. This large book is a wonderful compendium of ideas, real-life examples, resources, even recipes!

The Complete Idiot's Guide To Simple Living
By Georgene Lockwood

If you need a textbook for your curriculum of simplification, you need look no further. Georgene Lockwood has written the definitive book on the practicalities of it, with no nut nor bolt left out.

Category 9. Inspirational

Recommended: two titles:

Gift from the Sea
By Anne Morrow Lindbergh

While her pioneering exploits in the world of aviation are fading from public memory in these days of routine jet travel, this little gem of a book which Anne Morrow Lindbergh wrote while on vacation by the sea in the early 1950s continues to inspire generation after generation of people, particularly women. Listen to her speak:

"One learns first of all in beach living the art of shedding; how little one can get along with, not how much. Physical shedding to begin with, which then mysteriously spreads into other fields. Clothes, first. Of course, one needs less in the sun. But one needs less anyway, one finds suddenly. One does not need a closet-full, only a small suitcase-full. And what a relief it is! Less taking up and down of hems, less mending and – best of all – less worry about what to wear. One finds one is shedding not only clothes – but vanity.

Next, shelter. One does not need the airtight shelter one has in winter in the North. Here I live in a bare sea-shell of a cottage. No heat, no telephone, no plumbing to speak of, no hot water, a two-burner oil stove, no gadgets to go wrong. No rugs. There were some, but I rolled them up the first day. It is easier to sweep the sand off a bare floor. But I find I don't bustle about with unnecessary sweeping and cleaning here. I am no longer aware of the dust. I have shed my Puritan conscience about absolute tidiness and cleanliness. Is it possible that, too, is a material burden?"

No book list would be complete without this classic.

Adventures in Simple Living: A Creation-Centered Spirituality
By Richard Heffern

An inspirational book by a man with a deep commitment to simplicity at all levels. It is a small book – I read it in a day – but full of wisdom. Heffern shares his own feelings and experiences in a very intimate way and also pulls great quotes from dozens of other writers on the subject.

His is a wonderful example of how to move through the world with all your senses open and to savour what comes in. He writes:

"Attentive but relaxed, I walk just to hear the simple candor of the everyday, well lost and adrift on the meandering currents of an afternoon. If I am out just to see how spring or autumn is coming along, then a moment-by-moment waking up will ordinarily take place. The way the sunlight shines through oak leaves overhead as they dance and flutter in the winds, the feel of breezes across my neck and face, the honeysuckle smells mingled with the damp earth aroma, the magic music of a woodthrush heard in the distance, the broad blue blue skies and clouds overhead – these are the cues that prompt the awakening. Called insistently beyond myself, I am invited to open my eyes wider and wider to the world.

If I am out to think something through or in a meditative frame of mind, then slowly my thoughts will grow and ripen like the blackberries on the bushes alongside the trail."

Category 10. Other Recommended Titles

Dematerializing: Taming the Power of Possessions
By Jane Hammerslough

Jane's unusual book is about, as she puts it, "The power we seek from possessions and its repercussions on other areas of our lives".

In the late 1950s, TV was coming into every home and post-war materialism was getting into high gear. New ideas were revolutionizing the marketing industry. "Don't sell the product:" they were saying, "sell the vision, sell the dream, sell the achievement."

Nearly half a century later, our entire culture has been subjected to that message so thoroughly and for so long that it has penetrated deep into our unconscious minds. If we reason it out, we know perfectly well that a certain make of car or a certain designer label on a shirt is not going to make us better, sexier, cleverer or more successful people. But now that everyone has ingested the message, we all find ourselves playing it out, like so many puppets on the advertiser's string. We are making it come true!

Dematerializing is a painstaking examination of this whole phenomenon. The art of dematerializing our lives is to **"question what we really want and need in our own hearts"**. This is an excellent book for anyone (and that is most of us) who feels the seduction of possessions, of competition, and the promise of a material Nirvana.

Slowing Down to the Speed of Life: How to Create a More Peaceful, Simpler Life from the Inside Out
By Richard Carlson

Richard Carlson, author of the popular *Don't Sweat the Small Stuff* and other homespun, self-help titles, has written this one just on the topic of slowing down. He repeats the title phrase, "slowing down to the speed of life", so many times in the book that even though I was somewhat critical of the repetition, the idea behind it definitely did lodge in my brain, to good effect.

Don't Just Do Something: Sit There
By Sylvia Boorstein

If you want a Time Out Experience that costs nothing, have yourself a two-day (or longer) retreat right there where you live. Sylvia will explain exactly how, complete with timetable for each day.

For more resources, including a host of electronic ones, visit
www.lilypadlist.com

The Lilypad List

A checklist of reminders that will KEEP your life simple

1. Everything is Perfect:
No need to play the blame game – including self-blame
Remember: *There are no mistakes, only outcomes*

2. Time Out is Essential:
Keep 'alone time,' space and silence always in your life
Remember: *Set aside weeks per year, hours per week, minutes per day*

3. Sensory Awareness is the Key to Delight:
Keep coming to your senses
Remember: *We are all hunter-gatherers in our genes*

4. We Can Trust the Process:
Flow with the river of life, whatever happens
Remember:
Change and uncertainty are inevitable. It is just a dance of energy

5. We Are All Cells of the Living Earth:
Always think like a molecule
Remember: *What is good for the cell is good for the planet*

6. We All Make A Difference:
By living simply, you are making a difference
Remember: *Be the change you want to see happen in the world*

7. There Is Only the Now Moment:
Learn and practise mindfulness
Remember: *When you stay in the now, the simple life is a simple matter*

May you walk in beauty.

"The Miracle"

The blossom is on the blackthorn, and the garden is full of daffodils. The Earth is waking up.

I have walked past the pond many times these past few weeks, dragging bags of compost to fork into the beds I am digging over in readiness to receive the new season's seedlings. But until now, I have not stopped to look. So I pause in my work and squat down. Nothing much is happening. Not even the water boatmen and pond skaters are abroad on this cool, cloudy day.

Suddenly, I see the lovers.

They are hanging there, quietly, dreamily, motionless in the still water, the female below and the smaller male on top, his arms clasped around her waist. A cloud has formed behind them, and even as I watch, the cloud expands, each transparent egg, with its small, black nucleus, swelling in the water around the water parsnip stems.

Finally I have witnessed it, the silent annual miracle in my pond; I am so glad I looked.

There will be new frogs again this year. And I know that as long as there are frogs, there is hope.

Appendix A
"Free Therapy"
A simple method for understanding and dealing
with your emotional issues.

The Virtual Therapist

First, invent yourself a "virtual therapist".

Yes, I'm serious. Imagine the absolutely perfect listener – someone who will listen intently and compassionately to everything and
anything you say to him or her, without criticism, judgement or
blame, and will respond with unconditional love, respect and kind-
ness. Then act the role of that person as authentically as you possibly can.

Remember *never* to judge when in the role of the therapist.
Always be kind. Always have total compassion for your "client".

All this virtual therapist will ever do is listen, ask kind but prob-
ing questions, encourage you to go deeper, occasionally sum up for
you, keep you on track with the topic and reassure you that you are
not only not crazy but are actually saner than sane. Now make a
contract with this therapist that you will consult him/her whenever
there is anything about yourself or your life that you need help in
exploring.

Your therapist should have a voice; I talk with mine out loud
while I am out walking through the woods and lanes. This is more
difficult in the city but can still be done, even if you have to talk in
whispers. (Just don't do it on a bus or train, though, or you'll get
very odd looks.) If you are home alone, you can have your therapy
sessions indoors. By yourself in your car might work, but park it
first. If you are never alone, it can be done silently, but it is more difficult. The other alternative, if talking aloud is too tricky, is to have
a written dialogue, although that process takes longer.

Here are some of the useful phrases your therapist might use:
"Can you tell me more about this feeling?"
"Whereabouts in your body do you feel this most intensely?"
"Pretend you are only seven years old. If you were just to blurt out
what you really, truly feel/think/want right now, what would you
say?"

"Does this remind you of anything? When have you felt like this before?"

"Is there a familiar pattern happening here?"

"What does your 'inner child' have to say about this?"

"Can you tell me your ideas about what might need to change and how we might set about changing it?"

If change is indicated, use the four-step "brainstorm" method:

1. Make a note of *all possible* options, without evaluating them

2. Evaluate each one and make a short list

3. Choose the best

4. Figure out how to implement it

There are three other "self-therapy" techniques which could be useful:

Notice OTT reactions.

Do you ever find yourself suddenly reacting much more strongly and emotionally than the situation seems to warrant? "Over the top" emotional reactions are a sure sign that a deep nerve in you has been touched. Watch for these OTT reactions in your everyday life, and if one happens, take the next available opportunity to discuss it with your virtual therapist. Trace it back to its true origins (often in childhood).

Notice substitutions

Most of us tend to plaster over unbearable feelings with slightly more bearable ones. If we grew up in a family where anger was unacceptable, for example, whenever we feel anger we might speedily plaster sadness or depression on top of it, to hide it from ourselves. Some people paste laughter on top of the urge to weep. Teasing is frequently a cover for hostility.

It is easier to spot substitutions in other people than in ourselves, but if you are observant, you might catch a tiny glimpse of an original feeling just before it gets plastered over. Then with the help of your virtual therapist you can explore what is going on.

Use Two-Chair dialogues

Gestalt therapists use these a lot. They are useful if you have "unfinished business" with someone, e.g. an ex-partner or even a deceased parent. Imagine the other party sitting opposite you in a chair and address that person as though he or she were truly there. If you want to have a go at acting the part of the other and responding, swap chairs. Continue the dialogue, swapping chairs each time.

This is also useful for dialogues between two warring parts of yourself – e.g. the one who wants to simplify and the one putting up objections. It is a wonderful technique to use whenever you feel ambivalent about something. Be sure to keep the two sides of the equation in their correct chairs and to swap chairs each time you change "sides". Tune into your feelings in each chair and note if you prefer one over the other.

Bon voyage!

A word of caution:
These are powerful techniques, and should only be used by people in excellent mental health. It is unwise to use them if you have ever experienced a psychotic break or been diagnosed with a major psychiatric disorder such as schizophrenia. If you are already in therapy of any kind, tell your therapist about this extra "homework".

Appendix B
Get to know your ecological footprint

(Reprinted with permission from the Quaker Living Witness Project)

What is a fair share of the earth's resources? What should be your priorities for living more lightly? One way to get to grips with these questions is to work out your "ecological footprint", the area of land needed to support your lifestyle. This questionnaire will calculate your footprint score in "ares" of land, *based on global average land pro-ductivity levels*. One are is 100 square metres, or one hundredth of a hectare. That's a patch of land about ten paces by ten paces. The measurement isn't precise and may not fit your lifestyle perfectly; *please do be creative and make guesses, but be honest with yourself!*

1. FOOD

Accounts for land, energy and material use for food production, transport, processing and storage. Packaging is accounted for later, under waste.

Start with a score (based on a typical British diet, 38% animal-based) of   **155**

Serious meat eaters (50% animal-based diet)	add 25
Vegetarians (20% animal-based)	subtract 50
Vegans (0% animal-based)	subtract 100
If you only eat processed and/or imported food	add 5
If you eat 75% local, unprocessed food	subtract 10
If you only eat local, unprocessed food	subtract 15
If you only, or mostly, eat organic food	subtract another 10

    Your food score ____

2. WHERE YOU LIVE

Allows for land used by buildings, concrete, paving and grass, but not areas managed for wildlife or food. Also includes land use to provide construction materials, access roads, etc.

For a typical British semi, score	45
For a larger detached house	60
For a terraced house	35

| For a two-bedroom flat | 20 |
| For a studio | 10 |

Divide by no. of occupants to get your score

Your "where you live" score ____

3. TRANSPORT

Accounts for energy use, land use and materials for roads, materials and energy for vehicle manufacture, etc.

a) If you are a regular car user or passenger please score:

For high mileage drivers (15,000 miles/year alone)	200
For typical drivers (8,500 miles/year, with a passenger 40% of the time)	70
If you travel mainly as a car passenger score	30

But if most of your car trips are local (3 miles or less) add 25% to allow for extra energy use for cold starts.

These figures are based on UK average car fuel consumption of 8.5 litres/100km. If you drive a 4x4 (e.g. Range Rover Discovery) or MPV (e.g. Renault Espace), add 50%. For a small car (e.g. Clio or new Mini), subtract a third.

Your car score ____

b) If you use public transport:

For a weekly, 150-miles return trip by rail or bus, or a daily return commute of 30 miles score	20
c) If you only walk or cycle score	2
d) For each hour per year you spend flying, add	15

Your transport score (a+b+c+d) ____

4. MATERIAL SUPPLY AND WASTE

Accounts for energy and material use in manufacturing and construction, as well as land use and greenhouse gas emissions in waste disposal.

If you put out the UK average of 20kg a week (one dustbin-full of mixed waste including glass, food waste, etc.,) for the standard waste collection, score   430

If you recycle all glass and metal, and compost all food and garden waste, your rubbish for the standard collection may be mostly plastic bags, etc. and so much lighter. Score 22 points for each non-recycled kg per week.

For each kg per week of recycling, add   5

(1kg=2-3 wine bottles or 20 cans or 2 weekend papers or 10 weekday broadsheet papers)

For each kg per week of waste composted, score   0

If you filled a skip this year with building waste, score another   150

Divide the total by the number of people in your house to get your total waste score.

Your waste score _____

5. ENERGY IN YOUR HOME

Accounts for land use in energy supply, and greenhouse gas emissions from fossil fuel use.

First estimate your heating and hot water score.

A lot depends on the size of your home. To start off with:

If you live in a detached house, score   165

If you live in a semi-detached house, score   105

If you live in a terraced house   65

If you live in a flat   50

How warm is your home? For each degree above 17°C add 10%; for each degree below, subtract 10%.

If your home is well-insulated (e.g. a modern house with 200mm loft insulation, cavity wall insulation and double glazing), subtract 30%. If you have a new condensing-flue boiler subtract another 20%. If your boiler is over 15 years old add 15%.

If you don't have central heating and only heat one or two rooms in your home, score 50.

These figures are for gas. If you use electric heating, multiply your total by 2.5. If you use oil add 40%. For coal, add 80%. Now divide by the number of people living in the house

    Your heating and hot water score: _____

And now, your score for appliances. Start with a score of   40

If you only choose "A"-rated appliances and energy-efficient light bulbs,   subtract 10

If you are frugal in your use of appliances (switching off lights only

using the washing machine when full, not using a dishwasher or
clothes drier)   subtract 5
If you have a house full of energy-hungry people, with TVs on all
the time and daily use of a washing machine and dryer,   add 35
Divide by the number of people in the house.
If you use renewable electricity, divide by ten for your final appliances score:

**Now add up your score for heating & hot water and appli-
ances to get your home energy score _____**

6. EVERYTHING ELSE

*Accounts for land use and greenhouse gas emissions linked to provid-
ing services.*

Add up the amount (in £) you spend **each month** on the following:
Telecommunications – your share of the phone bill, mobile phone,
internet access, leisure and cultural activities (cinema, concerts, theatre, health club, visits to museums), etc. Restaurants, cafés and
hotels.
Divide by five to get a footprint score
Add 10 to allow for miscellaneous purchases and services such as
health and education.

Your "everything else" score ____

7. AT LAST – ADDING IT ALL UP

Add up your score for:
>   Food
>   Where you live
>   Transport
>   Materials and waste
>   Energy in your home
>   Everything else
>   **To get your total: ____**

How do you compare?

The amount of land available globally is 1.9ha (allowing for a
footprint score of 190)

Footprint scores around the world are:

Global average: 230 per person

India: 80 per person

United States: 970 per person

The UK average is 550 per person

The average Oxfordshire inhabitant scores 750

Londoners score 660

The Welsh score 525

Liverpudlians average 415

Copyleft: Living Witness Project, 20th October 2003, using data from Best Foot Forward, the Environmental Change Institute, and UK government statistics. Funding from Joseph Rowntree Charitable Trust gratefully acknowledged.
This questionnaire is under continuing development! If you have any comments or suggestions, please get in touch with Laurie Michaelis on 01865 302907, or at laurie.michaelis@eci.ox.ac.uk

Bibliography

ANDREWS, C. *Circle of Simplicity: Return to the Good Life.* New York: Harper, 1997.

ASLETT, D. *Clutter's Last Stand: It's Time to De-Junk Your Life.* Cincinnati: Writer's Digest Books, 1984.

BECK, C. J. *Everyday Zen: Love and Work.* San Francisco: Harper, 1989.

—*Nothing Special: Living Zen.* New York: Harper,1995.

BERRY, T. *The Great Work: Our way into the future.* New York: Random House, 1999.

BOORSTEIN, S. *Don't Just Do Something – Sit There.* San Francisco: Harper, 1996.

BRIERLEY, John. *A Pilgrim's Guide to the Camino Frances.* Findhorn: Camino Guides, 2003

CALLENBACH, E. "The Green Triangle." *In Context #26*, Summer 1990, Page 13.

CARLSON, R. & BAILEY, J. *Slowing Down to the Speed of Life: How to create a more peaceful, simpler life from the inside out.* London: Hodder, 1998.

CHRISTIAN, D. L. *Creating a Life Together.* Canada: New Society Publishers, 2003.

CSIKSZENTMIHALYI, M. Flow: *The Psychology of Optimal Experience.* New York: Harper, 1991.

ELGIN, D. *Voluntary Simplicity.* New York: William Morrow, 1998

ELKIN, B. *Simplicity & Success.* Canada: Trafford Publishing, 2003.

FELDMAN, C. *The Buddhist path to simplicity: spiritual practice for everyday life.* London: Thorsons, 2001.

FROMM, E. *To Have or To Be?* London: Continuum, 2000.

GHAZI, P. & JONES, J. *Downshifting: the guide to happier, simpler living.* London: Coronet, 1997.

HAMMERSLOUGH, J. *Dematerializing: Taming the Power of Possessions.* New York: Perseus Publishing, 2001.

HEFFERN, R. *Adventures in simple living: a creation-centered spirituality.* New York: Crossroad, 1994.

LINDBERGH, A. M. *Gift From the Sea*. New York: Pantheon Books, 1955.

LOCKWOOD, G. *The Complete Idiot's Guide to Simple Living*. Indianapolis: Alpha Books, 2000.

LUHRS, J. *The Simple Living Guide: A Sourcebook for Less Stressful, More Joyful Living*. New York: Broadway Books, 1997.

PIERCE, L. B. *Choosing Simplicity: Real People Finding Peace and Fulfillment in a Complex World*. Carmel, CA: Gallagher Press, 2000.

RAY, P. & ANDERSON, S. *The Cultural Creatives: How 50 million people are changing the world*. New York: Three Rivers Press, 2000.

ROBÈRT, K-H. *The Natural Step Story*. Canada: New Society Publishers, 2003.

SCHWARZ, W. & D. *Living Lightly: travels in post-consumer society*. Charlbury, Oxon: Jon Carpenter, 1998.

SINETAR, M. *Ordinary People as Monks and Mystics: Lifestyles for Self-discovery* Mahwah, NJ: Paulist Press, 1986.

TOLLE, E. *The Power of Now*. London: Hodder, 1999.

Index

Also by Marian Van Eyk McCain

Elderwoman promises that whoever sets out on her "third age" journey in a spirit of curiosity and awareness, consciously aligning herself with the natural processes of aging – and with the rhythms of the natural world around her – will discover unexpected richness, new kinds of power, freedom, and ever deepening joy, as she grows at last into her full potential as a woman and becomes a true elder, a spiritual leader for her times.

"In Elderwoman, Marian Van Eyk McCain charts the journey of growing old with optimism, joy and deep understanding. In our youth-orientated culture, this book is a breath of fresh air for those of us over the age of fifty."

—Christiane Northrup, M.D., author of Women's Bodies, Women's Wisdom

ISBN 1-899171-29-0 • available from www.findhornpress.com

About the Author

Marian Van Eyk McCain, author of *Transformation through Menopause* (Bergin & Garvey 1991), and *Elderwoman: reap the wisdom – feel the power – embrace the joy* (Findhorn Press, 2002), holds degrees in social work and east-west psychology and was for many years a transpersonal psychotherapist, workshop leader and health educator.

Her writing – on topics ranging from women's health and spirituality, personal growth, wellness, and stress-management to environmental politics, organic growing and alternative technology – has been widely published. She also writes poetry and short fiction.

You can contact Marian via the Internet at:
www.elderwoman.org or www.lilypadlist.com

About the Illustrator

Iris Hill is an Australian wildlife artist and conservationist with a lifelong love of Nature. Her exquisite works in coloured pencil have found a place in many Australian and overseas collections.